THE
FOUR-THIRDS
SOLUTION

Other books by Stanley I. Greenspan, M.D.

The Irreducible Needs of Children
(coauthor T. Berry Brazelton, M.D.)

Building Healthy Minds (with Nancy Breslau Lewis)

The Growth of the Mind (with Beryl Lieff Benderly)

The Child with Special Needs
(coauthor Serena Wieder, Ph.D., with Robin Simon)

Infancy and Early Childhood: The Practice of Clinical Assessment and Intervention with Emotional and Developmental Challenges

Developmentally Based Psychotherapy

The Challenging Child (with Jacqueline Salmon)

Playground Politics (with Jacqueline Salmon)

First Feelings (with Nancy Thorndike Greenspan)

The Essential Partnership
(with Nancy Thorndike Greenspan)

The Clinical Interview of the Child
(with Nancy Thorndike Greenspan)

The Development of the Ego

Psychopathology and Adaptation in Infancy and Early Childhood

Intelligence and Adaptation: An Integration of Psychoanalytic and Piagetian Developmental Psychology

A Consideration of Some Learning Variables in the Context of Psychoanalytic Theory

The Course of Life—Infancy to Aging, 7 volumes (coeditor)

Infants in Multi-Risk Families (coeditor)

Infancy: Handbook of Child and Adolescent Psychiatry (coeditor)

THE
FOUR-THIRDS
SOLUTION

*Solving the Child-Care Crisis
in America Today*

STANLEY I. GREENSPAN, M.D.
with Jacqueline Salmon

A Merloyd Lawrence Book

PERSEUS
PUBLISHING

Library of Congress catalog number for this book is available.

ISBN: 0-7382-0200-2
Copyright © 2001 by Stanley I. Greenspan, M.D.

Text design by Jeffrey P. Williams
Set in 11-point ITC Legacy Serif

1 2 3 4 5 6 7 8 9 10—03 02 01
First printing, October 2000

Perseus Publishing is a member of the Perseus Books Group.
Find us on the World Wide Web at http://www.perseuspublishing.com
Perseus Publishing books are available at special discounts for bulk purchases in the U.S. by corporations, institutions, and other organizations. For more information, please contact the Special Markets Department at the Perseus Books Group, 11 Cambridge Center, Cambridge, MA 02142, or call (617) 252-5298 or email j.mccrary@perseusbooks.com.

Contents

❊ PART THREE:
WHERE DO WE GO FROM HERE?

To Elizabeth, Jake, and Sarah
and the many other young adults
who will be rearing future generations.
—S.G.

To Tim, Sarah, and Chris
all my love.
—J.S.

THE
FOUR-THIRDS
SOLUTION

PART ONE

What's at Stake

1

Our Social Experiment

When asked what they most want for their children, many parents might say happiness in their children's personal lives and success in their careers. Asked about the qualities their children would need to achieve such happiness and success, parents might mention an optimistic outlook on life and the fortitude to bounce back from the inevitable challenges that they will face. Elaborating their wishes further, parents might hope that their children would develop reflective thinking and the ability to develop warm, intimate relationships with other people.

These capacities lie at the core of our humanness. They are the roots from which our communities and our society grow and blossom. Though we often take them for granted, they allow us to create nurturing families and to work cohesively in groups and communities. Without these capacities, we would find ourselves functioning on a much less healthy basis—acting impulsively, jumping to quick, often extreme, conclusions, and becoming increasingly self-centered or passive and helpless.

Many readers know that the ability to love, nurture others, think, and be aware of their own and others' feelings depends on growing up in warm, caring, sensitive relationships with reliable parents. Intimacy, empathy, and dependency rest partly on having our needs met in a warm and nurturing manner. It's hard to give of ourselves in a deep and meaningful way if others have not done the same for us. In addition, as I have shown in an earlier book, *Building Healthy Minds*, the roots of thinking are also in early experience, in intimate exchanges in which emotional signals are sent back and forth over long stretches of time. These provide practice in recognizing the intention of another person and the ability to be part of a creative, logical dialogue.

Try to imagine a society in which one half of the babies and young children spent most of their waking hours away from their parents and in the care of others, many of whom were poorly trained, overworked, and underpaid and were caring for more children than anyone could realistically nurture. Because of these circumstances, few of these children received much one-on-one attention, warmth, cuddling, and interactions. If one visited the child-care centers in this hypothetical society, one would see that the children generally were clean and fed. But only rarely did they experience those games so common in families, where babies and parents exchange flirtatious looks, make silly faces at each other, or exchange expressive gestures about food, toys, or mutual feelings. Would you expect children who grew up in these circumstances to be able to nurture and rear children warmly themselves? Would they be able to handle frustration with thoughtful and reflective thinking and to work together with empathy and compassion?

Obviously, we're not dealing with a hypothetical society. At present, out-of-home child care in our society has grown dramatically since 1970. At present, almost 13 million infants, toddlers, and preschoolers—more than half of our nation's 21 million preschool population—are receiving care from someone other than their parents or another family member. More than half of these child-care children spend 35 hours a week or more in day care, and more than one third are in two or *more* child-care arrangements each week.[1] Our society has launched into a monumental experiment that has the potential to change who we are and how we function as individuals and therefore how our communities and, indeed, how our society will work in the future.

It's difficult to discuss this worrisome dilemma because, as we all know, child-care is tied to many other sensitive issues, such as gender equality, family income levels, and even welfare reform. And yet, as recent research has shown, our societal experiment isn't going well. As we will discuss in Chapter 2, a growing number of studies indicate that most of our children are being cared for in child-care centers and other out-of-home arrangements that have significant limitations. In fact, most studies that have examined the availability of quality child care in this country have come to the same grim conclusion: Most of the child care available for infants and toddlers in this country simply isn't of high quality.

We often try to reassure ourselves that there are day-care providers and centers that do provide good nurturing, but the vast majority of institutional or family day care is not of high quality and, furthermore, is poorly regulated. It's important to point out early in this discussion, however, that the dilemma in child care is not parents' fault, and in many respects it's not the fault of child-care providers either. As I will show in Chapter 2, we may simply be asking the day-care system to do too much: We are expecting it to operate the way very well-functioning families do. But most out-of-home care can't give a child what a well-functioning family is designed to provide. Even at the best centers, caregivers in the infant rooms usually care for four or more babies, and child-to-staff ratios for toddlers can rise as high as 10 to 1. What's more, caregivers may change rapidly because of high turnover in the child-care field and because of child-care center practices that dictate that children be moved from one room to another as they grow. As a result, children aren't getting the consistent, one-on-one nurturing with the same caregiver over a long period of time that almost all of us who study and work with children agree they need. Furthermore, many highly motivated caregivers don't receive the training, support, and pay they need to work with children on a sustained basis.

I'm not pointing out these facts because I'm nostalgic for the days when fewer women worked outside the home. I believe that both parents should have equal opportunities to pursue their careers. In fact, we're all very aware that economic realities mean that most families need two salaries. Hardworking parents need everyone's support, not more guilt. In Part Three of this book, I will discuss the ways in which child care can be improved for families that need it.

Nevertheless, we need to look realistically at the challenges of giving children what they need while allowing both parents to make ends meet and shape careers. If we can face the fact that most children in day-care settings are not getting the kinds of experiences and interactions they need for healthy growth, we are more likely to be able to work toward solutions. In this book, we will suggest solutions for the child-care dilemma that respect the equality of men and women as well as the economic necessities, while making the care of babies and toddlers a top priority.

In this and the next two chapters we will look more closely at the extent of our child-care dilemma. We'll compare what children need to develop optimally in our fast-moving, complex world with what child care currently provides them, and discuss the implications of this for the future evolution of society.

The Essentials of Childhood

Over the years, in my research and practice, I have learned much about how children grow emotionally and intellectually and the ways in which they develop the traits that are critically important in adulthood. We've discovered that children move through stages, or milestones, in their first three years. We can even pinpoint in some detail certain emotional interactions that must occur between children and those who care for them at each stage of their development if they are to master these milestones.

In other words, we are beginning to sketch out the road map to the development of an intelligent, creative, logical, can-do person who can think in abstractions and solve tough problems and yet also be nurturing and empathetic. We now know that such individuals have experienced specific types of emotional interactions. We've been able to divide these critical experiences into six stages. In addition, the elusive moral compass we all so desperately want for our children appears to develop from these same emotional interactions. Our children's sense of self, as well as their self-esteem, also blossom as a result of traveling this rich journey with their parents.

Some of these interactions take place in the seemingly silly make-believe games we play with babies in which we pretend to be their horse or favorite bunny. During an infinite number of subtle, day-to-day encounters, we tune into our infants', toddlers', and preschoolers' emotional reactions to the world with our own emotional chemistry. In Chapter 3, we'll show how the fun games that parents naturally play with their children support all six of the important stages that build healthy minds.

This journey is not all fun and games. Some of the important interactions take place during the difficult times of parenting: When we're in the trenches, struggling to deal with a small child's stubbornness, anger, or willfulness or cuddling and rocking them because they're irritable or upset, we are giving them priceless lessons.

The most important point to remember is this: The essential ingredient needed to grow intelligence, morality, intimacy, empathy, sense of self, and self-esteem in our children is not educational toys, nursery school classes, trips, tutoring, or the extracurricular activities that fill our schedules and those of our children to the brim. The key ingredient is regular, substantial doses of *us*. The hours we devote each day, each week, each month, each year to every imaginable type of intimate interaction with babies and small children—through pretend play, empathetically reading their emotional signals and moods, debating with them, satisfying their curiosity about the world, guiding them within the structure of firm values and limits—all of these go toward this ultimate goal of raising a warm, intelligent, moral human being. Our children require our minds, our presence, and souls. In practical terms, this means they require more of us than our busy society encourages.

Knowing what we want for our children, and knowing that it can't be provided on the run or through special weekend outings or even on the most wonderful vacations, but only in extended intimacies every day, brings us face-to-face with the reality of our child-care system. Will children growing up in institutional day care as we know it today learn to be caring, loving, empathetic, creative, reflective adults?

Priorities

Recently, I saw an automobile advertisement in a magazine that neatly summed up the lofty expectations we have in our society. "If life came with a report card, you'd be bringing home straight A's," the ad cooed. "Career: A+. Family: A+. All around your life is pretty good. After all, you pride yourself in making educated choices." By owning a particular brand of car, the ad assured readers, "you can add another class to your report card of life. Car: A+."

Unfortunately, this ad is a stunningly accurate portrayal of the state of our culture these days. Highly successful people are defined as those who achieve top grades in every aspect of their lives: in career, family, physical appearance, psyche—as well as in car purchases. Along with a high-flying, top-paying career, to which we must be completely devoted, we are also expected to have high-achieving spouses, academically successful children, a rich social life, a physically fit body, and a healthy psyche that we've honed with personal-improvement programs. Millions of us are pushing ourselves (and our children) harder and harder to achieve those A+ grades in every aspect of our lives.

By aiming for complete satisfaction or success in career and work, we often end up stealing time away from the rich emotional life that can offer us true sustenance and satisfaction. The deep sense of belonging and contentment that comes from an intimate involvement with our spouses, our children, our communities doesn't come by sprinting through a crowded schedule of work and social activities. The fact is, we can't achieve A+ grades in every aspect of our lives, even though our culture keeps telling us we can. Indeed, earning an A+ at work may carry the price of a D- in family life and child rearing. Because the results of child rearing are often not apparent for many years after a child has left the nest, or may be hidden in the child's deepest feelings, many parents won't even know what the impact of their priorities turns out to be.

Today's economic forces are stretching our emotional bonds almost to the breaking point. Many parents see no choice but to have both parents in the workforce. Millions of families—including single-parent families and those earning low hourly wages—must work ever longer hours in order to put bread on the table.

In many ways, our move away from deeply cemented familial ties and our growing reliance on outside services in almost every aspect of our lives is a new experience for our culture. For much of our past, children grew up amid a network of close interactions with adults. They lived in tribes, villages, or small country towns, surrounded by people who knew them and whom they knew intimately. Many families lived with extended family members—grandparents, maybe some aunts and uncles—under one roof or in close proximity. We had close ties to our neighbors and to our community. Families often stayed in one area for many generations. If they moved, as was the practice in our pioneer days, families pulled together into close communities as they traveled. In cities, they spent most of their lives within neighborhoods.

It would be easy to say that I'm idealizing our past. Indeed, many scholars believe that our modern culture has a distorted view of how families operated in the past, particularly when it comes to the issue of whether mothers were more able to care for children full-time than is currently the case. Volumes have been written about the subject and debates continue. Nonetheless, the current social experiment, where middle- and upper-middle-income families who can afford it use institutions outside the home to care for their infants and toddlers is a significant departure from very recent history. The nannies or nursemaids of the past, who were stable figures for many years in the families who could afford them, often did the consistent, one-on-one nurturing that we are talking about here.

As will be discussed in subsequent chapters, we are asking too much from our child-care system. Millions of parents are seeking services from an industry that isn't equipped to provide quality care to all those children. As stated, this isn't parents' fault, and we all need to be aware of the problem so we can be part of the solution. Children's needs must be the top priority in *both* parents' career and financial decisions.

With two-career families, high divorce rates, many single parents, and increasing numbers of parents with more than one job, as well as fewer extended-family households, children have fewer and fewer opportunities to develop warm, close ties to the adults in their lives. As a result, there is a danger that we will see more self-centered, impulsive, or passive, and hopeless children or young adults than in the past.

Unfortunately, there are already worrisome signs that children are struggling in this new world. The United States has the highest rate of childhood homicide, suicide, and firearms-related deaths of any of the world's 26 richest nations.[2] The murder rate for children has tripled since 1950, and though the suicide rate among children has dropped from a record high in the early 1990s, it is still one of the leading causes of death for young people in the U.S. Obesity among children has doubled in the last 20 years.

Shifting our priorities does not mean restricting one parent to staying home during the years that children are growing up. It does not mean a return to a hierarchical household in which Father is the sole breadwinner and Mother supplies all the love and attention. Genuine "family values" that center on the importance of intimate interactions do not mean that every parent must conform to historically rigid roles. Rather, it means acknowledging and accepting a joint responsibility for the consistent nurturing of babies and small children.

Parents should not have to shoulder this responsibility alone. Our culture also needs to accept its share of responsibility for supporting parents. Right now, society simply assumes that raising children is parents' private concern. The tax structure, governmental policies, employment practices, even popular culture assumes that the rearing of the next generation is parents' private concern.

The Evolutionary Danger

In order to anticipate the impact of this social experiment, we need to take a good look at the potential effects of our current child-rearing patterns. We need to ask whether, by endangering children's access to crucially important early emotional experiences, we are in danger of changing the character structure of future adults. We need to inquire whether giving up the care of our children to others is a possible turning point in our evolution, especially if we view the ability to nurture and care for others as essential to the development of a complex society.

I believe that the consequences of depriving children of key early emotional experiences are grave. Many of those who don't get sufficiently sensitive early emotional caregiving may act impulsively and think in rigid, polarized terms. We have seen children, for example, who pull out knives and guns to settle a dispute over something as minor as a jacket. Such children may also have difficulty recognizing nuance and subtlety in the world. When someone disagrees with them—whether over a scored run or an opinion—they assume that the person "hates me" or vice versa. Additionally, they may ignore the rights, needs, and dignity of others. If the number of such individuals rises, then we can expect society to become more unpredictable and dangerous, with rising violence and antisocial behavior and less self-restraint and negotiation. Other children may grow up to be passive and depressed. There is also a danger of self-absorption—withdrawing from our communities and becoming focused solely on one's own concrete needs, such as food, clothing, and base-level excitement.

The impersonality of our lives brought on by social and technological changes threatens the very abilities that have made progress possible. The qualities most closely identified with our humanity—reason, compassion, love, intuition, intelligence, creativity, courage, morality, spirituality—develop from the interplay between the individual nervous system and the emotional experience of daily interactions. Without these experiences, future generations will be less able truly to empathize and care for each other and also less capable of raising children, maintaining families, solving complex problems, and working together in groups.

It would be easy to downplay this evolutionary danger and take for granted our reflective thinking and our ability to support our complex society. But the lack of these qualities would be sorely felt. For example, when neighbors argue over the height of a fence or the barking of a dog, they need to be able to continue to be civil and work together in ways to help their community while they work out their differences. A stable society depends upon the ability to reflect together in groups and find reasoned positions that can bring together different viewpoints, such as when communities work together to resolve such issues as building new schools, curbing pollution, and setting tax levels. Part of the capacity for reflective thinking is possessing a sufficient degree of self-awareness to take a step away from one's own biases or extreme viewpoints (which we all have but don't necessarily act upon). It is an ability both to be aware of our own emotions and to look at a problem from many angles.

If we look at conditions around the world and at the dysfunctional way that many adults are operating, it's easy to sense that we are balanced rather precariously. Many of us worry that this balance can tip—not only in individuals but also in groups. Sometimes whole societies can tip toward polarized rather than reflective solutions. Indeed, each and every day in our current society, we see polarized conflict between individuals who hold extreme and fixed outlooks. We see impulsive behavior and aggression. We also see passivity and helplessness—expressed as, for example, more depression among children and adults and large numbers of children who are retreating from the world through drug and alcohol use.

It's taken us a long time to build family and community structures that can support high-level mental abilities. Indeed, given what we now know about the experiences necessary for reflective and abstract thought, intimacy, and social cohesion, it is hard to imagine a design better than the family structure to teach these skills. When functioning well, it seems ideally suited to providing children with the needed emotional and social experiences. In fact, as will be seen in Chapter 3, the six types of experiences that appear to be essential for a healthy mind happen rather routinely and effortlessly in well-functioning families.

Because the family has always filled this important role, we need to inquire about the effect on child rearing of changing social patterns as well as new technologies. Will we continue to rear children to participate in the reflective thinking necessary for the continuation of stable communities and democratic institutions? We cannot assume that these abilities are so well established now that we can afford to give a few inches and still be secure!

No doubt some will argue that every new social change is initially met with fear and trepidation but that, over time, most people adapt to newly challenging situations. Those who do not adapt fall by the wayside, and a strong society emerges. Taken to the extreme, this position would be that whatever survives is, by definition, the fittest and therefore deserves to prevail on our evolutionary scale.

This point of view leaves out two important factors: the role of complex abilities in survival and our ability as human beings to shape our environment and institutions. The cockroach may be the only moving organism that would survive a nuclear holocaust. In the context of nuclear fallout, then, the cockroach is the fittest, and more complex living creatures would not survive. In the context of impersonal child rearing in large groups, an aggressive, self-centered child may adapt most easily to the setting at hand.

Living organisms do indeed tend to adapt to their settings. In many cases, the setting favors complex abilities. For example, climates that have seasonal changes favor creatures that can create dwellings to keep themselves warm. Those who can work with their hands to build such dwellings will have an added advantage. This assumption, however—that the setting will create challenges that support greater complexity of functioning, for example, learning to use tools—may not always be the case. As with the case of our cockroach, highly toxic settings may favor a simpler set of functions. Thus, compromised child rearing on a large scale may increase polarized, concrete thinking, passive hopelessness, or impulsivity rather than the empathetic, reflective thinking needed to sustain families and a complex society.

In addition, human society depends upon an ability to change our environment according to our needs, and to recognize when we are doing so in destructive ways. We are becoming more aware of this critical responsibility in such areas as global warming, nuclear proliferation, toxic waste, and the like, though many will argue that we're not doing enough in these areas. Our capacity to change our world through changing social patterns depends on the existence of individuals and groups capable of working together toward innovative future solutions—a tall order in today's social climate. Yet with biological, nuclear, or ecological dangers growing each year, more than ever the world needs empathetic, reflective individuals who can problem-solve and find new solutions. Against these needs, a new type of child-care arrangement that affects more than half the population and has the potential to create a less reflective type of person is especially risky. If such arrangements do indeed foster polarized and impulsive personalities, what implications will that have for the nature of future society?

Two Sides of Human Nature

From an evolutionary perspective, the task of protecting against self-destruction and that of promoting the organization that leads to more complex civilization, human families, and societies seem to have acquired, and required, two very important sets of abilities. One set has helped us master our environment. Clearly, this attribute was essential in our early years as humans. We needed to be able to hunt for food, protect ourselves from wild animals, make weapons, and defend territories. Without this assertive mastery of the forces arrayed against us, we easily could have faded away along with other now-extinct species.

These skills that help us master the world have served us well. This path of mastery at all costs has sent many businesspeople to the pinnacle of financial success and has also brought numerous economic and technological benefits to our society. But they can also be destructive. We have seen the dangers of aggression and damage to the environment. We can see it in the 100-hour-work-week mentality.

But evolution also has another path. In order to care for our young, to form close-knit societal structures and provide stability for ourselves, we needed to be able to go beyond simple survival and mastery of the environment. We learned to empathize with and adapt to the needs of others. Traits of nurturing and stewardship emerged. From this came intimate worlds of families, in which the tender love of attentive parents helps a child blossom and grow and adults can relax and show loving sympathy after a tough day at work.

Nowhere is this nurturing and empathetic side of our nature more important than when it comes to caring for newborn babies and children in the early years of their lives. It is this which allows one generation to pass intellectual, social, and emotional capacities to the next, and to give them the ability in turn to nurture their young. Our complex social structures involving families, communities, and various governmental institutions rely on this softer side of evolution. In fact, our capacity for nurturing and social cohesion provides the framework or structure within which the other side of our nature—competition, mastery of new challenges, including technology—can occur. All well-functioning groups, even successful armies, require this social cohesion in order to work together toward shared goals. In fact our ability to organize and work in groups is perhaps our species' most competitive advantage. We therefore come full circle. Survival of the fittest and nurturing are two sides of the same coin.

Part of what enables us to provide compassion and care for infants and young children is our capacity to appreciate their vulnerability and helplessness. For example, a daddy rocks his shrieking eight-month-old with calm reassurances. "Let's relax, buddy," he says while giving his child a gentle back rub until little Willie's crying eases and he heeds his dad's rhythmic message. This dad understands his son's utter vulnerability at a deep intuitive level and is therefore able to provide the appropriate empathetic care his son needs at that moment. How different is that scenario from a father who hears his son's crying as an irritating assault and hits or shakes him, which only frightens the child and increases his crying. "Damn it, listen to me," he shouts. "Be quiet!" The first father understands his child's vulnerability. The second father appears to mistake vulnerability for deliberate aggression or defiance.

Though most parents never reach the extreme of the second father, they can probably recall having those feelings—impatience at a crying child who doesn't seem to respond to attempts to offer comfort, exasperation at a baby who just won't cooperate and calm down, and anger that the child isn't aware that we are sick and tired of all that noise. Most of us, however, because of early experiences, have learned to control these reactions and maintain nurturing concern in the face of frustration.

The contrasting reactions to vulnerability can be seen in whole societies. When the vital balance between self-centered, competitive mastery of the environment and appreciation of others' vulnerability begins to favor the winner-take-all mentality and ignores the "chicken soup" that produces winners in the first place, society can regress to a more primitive level.

Today, driven by real or perceived economic necessity, we may have moved too far into the competitive side of adaptation, with 14-hour workdays and scraps of family time as we grasp for more and more material rewards and the pleasure we think they will bring. In doing so, we may be neglecting an equally adaptive side of our nature and compromising the quality of our society or even our long-term survival.

Why, at this point in our history, are we moving away from the traditional situation where parents provide the bulk of their children's care and also nurture each other, as well as other vulnerable members of society? My hunch is that our need to deny our own vulnerability and dependency makes us turn away from those who remind us of our condition. Because we see ourselves as totally independent and in control, we can't bear to see helplessness in our children and are therefore turning their care over to others.

Then one must ask why we are denying our own vulnerability and helplessness. One possibility is the following: In earlier periods of our history, we could split the nurturing side of our social fabric and the more aggressive mastery side into two different sets of cultural expectations. In the immediate past—say, up until the end of the nineteenth century—women embodied the first and men embodied the second. With the social changes of the last 75 years that have supported equality of opportunity for the sexes, it's no longer possible to create this convenient split. Now each person—whether a man or woman—must embody both of these important capacities: mastery and nurture.

In addition, we must now integrate these sides of life at a level of conscious choice, rather than expressing them by means of automatically prescribed social roles. The gift of conscious choice makes for more flexible adaptations, but it is also far more difficult.

This difficulty in reconciling the different facets of our humanity, now that the old splits are no longer possible, may itself be compounded by larger social and technological trends. Despite great strides in equalizing opportunities for both sexes, with men and women equally well educated and often equally well prepared for both professional success and caring for a family, new cultural expectations are pulling at us as well. Education is likely to take young adults away from their families of origin or extended families into new communities. New modes of communication, ranging from e-mail to videoconferencing, are pulling people even farther and farther away from the flesh-and-bones presence of their original nurturing groups. When we talk of a global world tied together by new forms of communication, travel, and technology, we at once generate both the need for greater interdependence and a greater isolation. If we put all these changes together, we see that they can be used to bring us closer together, such as flying to see our parents on the holidays, or farther apart, as in leaving family and friends and flying across the country for school or a new job. At the moment, it is fair to say that for most of us these advances have led to more isolation than closeness. Perhaps, like a new toy, these social and technological changes need to be played with for a while until we see that our seeming freedoms are not as necessary as our basic emotional and biological needs for nurturing and closeness. Of all these social changes, giving the rearing of our own children up to impersonal group care has the most repercussions. If we continue this experiment without examining the results, we may set in motion changes so dramatic and so permanent that we are unable to reverse course.

If society accepts inadequate institutional child care, we may well produce future generations incapable of demonstrating the nurturing side of our nature. Over time, those who dismiss the importance of this side of ourselves may be chagrined to discover that once you erode it, you also erode men's and women's ability to nurture future generations, work together in cohesive social organizations, and use reflection to solve technological and environmental challenges. That's because human beings, unlike most other creatures in the animal kingdom, have a very long period of helplessness and dependency. Without the vital balance between these two polarities of life, mastery and nurturance, we can't expect future generations to excel in either respect.

Whether or not this hypothesis—that we are neglecting one side of our human nature, the nurturing side—is correct in all aspects of our lives, the long-term consequences of farming out the care of almost half of our young children to nonfamily, institutional facilities is something we urgently need to examine.

What does all this mean to a couple expecting a child or to a family with young children? Right now, their choices often aren't attractive. If they choose to keep one parent at home all the time to care for the children, then they give up income and, perhaps, one parent's future career options. If both work at busy jobs, they have to give up precious moments with their children. Parents everywhere agonize about the choice. Which life do they pick?

In this book we will discuss this dilemma, and we ask readers to consider taking actions that aren't discussed a lot in our society, such as doing without some material possessions or perhaps rapid career advancement in order to clear enough space in your life for time with your children. Imperfectly and haltingly, many families are already making these wise choices to invest more of themselves in their children. We'll introduce parents who are doing this.

Obviously, for the millions of single parents and for couples who are both working just to put bread on the table, working less in order to create more time for their children may not be a realistic option. That's where government and industry come in. We should be asking them to consider changing their priorities so that it is easier for parents to make the choices that are best for their children.

This is a solvable problem, individually and collectively.

The central issue, then, isn't just whether day care is good or bad, important as this issue is. The central issue is the possibility of developing a new family ethic, a new view of how we raise our children and create citizens for a future society. In the following chapters, our book will lay out why and how we can put the care of our children, our family relationships, and the quality of emotional experience in the home first.

It is our human imperative.

2

We Are Asking
Too Much of Day Care

Unanswered questions

Who will care for my child while I am at work? Millions of working parents are asking just that question.

Can that person or child-care center provide what my child needs in order to develop into an intelligent, creative, morally sound adult?

What's best for my child?

These are crucial questions, and working parents everywhere wrestle with them.

Up until just a few years ago, most studies of day care that focused on differences between children who attended day care and children who were cared for exclusively at home by a mother found that day-care children were no different from at-home children when it came to cognitive and language development.

With these results in hand, many experts reassured parents that full-time day care was okay for infants and young children.

But more recent reports have focused on the *quality* of the day care and have looked more closely at children's emotional and social functioning. These studies provide a fuller picture than the earlier reports—and what we see is not reassuring. We are finding that the vast majority of child care is *not* of high quality. In addition, new research shows that many hours in day care (30 hours or more per week) is associated with increased problem behavior, especially aggressive behavior at age four and a half and in kindergarten, and that toddlers and preschoolers who spend all day in an out-of-home group child-care setting often show physiologic signs of stress such as high cortisol levels. Taken together, these findings raise serious questions about the earlier studies of child care and our comfortable assumption that full-time day care is all right for infants and young children.

Let's look at a fairly typical middle-class couple, Melinda and Robert. When they married, there was every indication that they would be good parents. They were warm and nurturing people, and they had a solid marriage. They also had plenty of experience with children. Melinda baby-sat as a teenager, and Robert was the oldest of a large family. They live in a community with fairly typical day-care options: several day-care centers that meet the state's minimally acceptable standards and a number of family child-care providers, some of whom are licensed by the state and some who are not.

But when Melinda, an accountant, was about five months pregnant, the question of who would care for her baby when she returned to work after a three-month maternity leave began to gnaw at her. She and Robert had the following conversation:

"I'm getting worried about what we're going to do with the baby when I go back to work."

"Really?" Robert replied. "I thought we'd decided all that. We're on the waiting list at that child-care center down the street from your office. It sounded pretty good."

"I just don't know," Melinda said uneasily. "I'm not happy with some of the stuff I've been reading about child care."

"About what?" said Robert. "The article you showed me said that kids in day care are okay in language skills and areas like that, just like children who aren't. Our friends who have children in day care seem to be pretty comfortable with it."

Melinda shook her head. "There seem to be lots of different answers, and I'm not sure who to believe. This book I'm reading says that kids in day care develop just the same as kids who aren't. But some people say day care is not so good for babies because they get sick a lot, and that they don't get the nurturing or stimulation they need."

Families like Melinda and Robert have every right to be confused. They have a very specific question: "What might be the effect on our child's development if we use the full-time day care that is available in our community? What should we do?"

What *is* best for our child?

In this chapter, we will try to answer that question by looking at the research and clinical observations on day care.

A Political Hot Potato

In recent years, the question of children and child care has become a hotly contested issue. Parents, researchers, politicians, commentators, and early-education and mental-health professionals have debated the effects of day care on the young children of millions of working parents. But despite all this talk, few of the professionals engaged in this debate have given people like Melinda and Robert clear answers to their questions and concerns about the health and safety and development of children in day care. One reason parents aren't getting straightforward information is because the issue of children and child care is an emotional one for everyone. Some parents may see any criticism about child care as an attack on their particular decisions: their choice of child care, their choice to work. Those who have devoted themselves to activism in the child-care field may see criticism as a commentary on their life's work. For others, the issue can take a liberal-versus-conservative cast: If you support day care, then you're liberal. And if you don't support day care, then you're a conservative. Also, criticism of day care has often been interpreted as an attack on mothers who work outside the home. The assumption is that critics of day care are really advocating a return to an era when women stayed at home and cared for children instead of pursuing careers.

These agendas become entwined in a tangle of confusion, and they are preventing us from having a coherent discussion about the actual quality of day care today and the question of whether millions of our children should be spending so much time at child-care centers or in family child-care providers' homes as they exist now.

If we clear away the smoke generated by the other issues, this is what we see: Much of the child care available for infants and toddlers in this country simply isn't good for them. Some will argue, correctly, that parents' care of their children varies widely, too, and all of us who are parents would certainly agree! Also, as we will discuss shortly, enriched child-care programs for *at-risk* children and families have been quite helpful. But neither of these facts allows us to ignore the problems in a system of child care being used by millions of children and families.

A growing body of recent research indicates that most of our children are being cared for in child-care centers and other out-of-home arrangements that have significant limitations. Most day care does not give a child consistent, sensitive, high-quality, nurturing care by one or a few caregivers. Even the best child-care situations often lack consistent staff and the capacity for the one-on-one nurturing that is needed—that is, continuity of the same nurturing caregiver over a number of years and with enough time for lots of sensitive nuances of emotional and social interactions. At less-than-adequate centers, children often lack even the most basic protection and physical care.

Evaluating Child Care

Many studies over the past decade confirm that high-quality child care is the exception rather than the rule among the child care available to most infants and children these days. In its voluminous report on early-childhood development, "From Neurons to Neighborhoods," the National Academy of Sciences reports that "child care that is available in the United States today is highly fragmented and characterized by marked variations in quality, ranging from rich, growth-promoting experiences to unstimulating, highly unstable and sometimes dangerous settings."[1]

This statement identifies the scope of the problem. A number of studies outline the magnitude of the challenge: Only about 9 to 15 percent of child care is of high quality. Here are some of those studies:

• A four-state study of 100 randomly chosen child-care centers found that the vast majority of children who spent their days in child-care centers were receiving less-than-adequate care.[2] "Most child care is mediocre in quality, [and] sufficiently poor to interfere with children's emotional and intellectual development," the researchers said in their final report. The study, conducted by four universities, examined centers in California, Colorado, Connecticut, and North Carolina. It rated 86 percent of the centers inspected "less than good." Put another way, just 14 percent—one in seven child-care centers—was rated as good quality.

Most troubling, according to this study, was the lower quality of care for very young children, where only 10 percent of the facilities were considered to be of high quality. "Babies in poor-quality rooms are vulnerable to more illness because basic sanitary conditions are not met for diapering and feeding; are endangered because of safety problems that exist in the room; miss warm, supportive relationships with adults; and lose out on learning because they lack the books and toys required for physical and intellectual growth," the study said.

• An ongoing federally funded study by the National Institute of Child Health and Human Development, where teams of investigators have been following 1,200 children of working and nonworking mothers since the early 1990s. In its sample, the NICHD found only 12 percent of child-care settings were of high quality, and when researchers analyzed their data to arrive at a national estimate, it was that 9 percent were of high quality.[3]

In this study, high-quality care was defined by the degree to which positive caregiving characterized the caregiver-child interactions. There were four ratings levels of the interactions, and percentages were calculated for out-of-home care (e.g., day care) for the United States as a whole. The four levels are:

Positive caregiving is *highly* characteristic—9 percent.
Positive caregiving is *somewhat* characteristic—
    30 percent.
Positive caregiving is *somewhat* uncharacteristic—
    53 percent.
Positive caregiving is *very* uncharacteristic—8 percent.

These findings have been characterized to mean that average care is "adequate." But the above breakdown indicates that questions need to be raised about whether settings where positive caregiving is "somewhat *un*characteristic" or only "somewhat *characteristic*" should be viewed as "adequate." Levels of quality in parental care have not yet been analyzed and broken down in this way, though the data are available.

In terms of overall trends, however, for children under the age of three, the NICHD report said, "The highest level of positive caregiving was provided by in-home caregivers, including fathers and grandparents caring for only one child, closely followed by home-based arrangements with relatively few children per adult."

• A study of family child-care providers found that the care provided in only 9 percent of the homes was of good quality. More than one third of the homes were considered of such poor quality that they were potentially harmful to a child's healthy growth, according to the study, conducted by the Families and Work Institute.[4]

• A study of 225 child-care centers in five cities and 65 towns in Southern California was conducted by the Child Care Employee Project, a California organization devoted to improving child care. It revealed that the quality of most child-care centers was "barely adequate when rated on such characteristics as staff-to-child ratios, harshness of staff toward children, and staff turnover. "The lowest quality was found in infant classrooms."[5]

• Most worrisome are recent reports of the quality of the child care for the 1 million children affected by the work requirements in the Personal Responsibility and Work Opportunity Reconciliation Act of 1996 ("welfare reform"). One study of the children of 1,000 mothers in three states who had placed their children in day-care centers and homes because of the welfare rules found very poor-quality care. Many children spent hours watching television, said the study, and researchers reported toddlers wandering aimlessly around without appropriate opportunities for nurturing interactions. In comparison to the earlier national studies of child-care quality (which, as we saw above, were not encouraging), the study from the University of California at Berkeley said the authors found "that children in the new welfare system have entered centers of even lower quality."[6]

Some may try to counter these findings by emphasizing the data on the benefits of work to parents and their children. Work may indeed have important benefits, but differences in children's development between working and nonworking poor parents can be accounted for by the mother's education, the family size, its ethnic group, and its psychological well-being rather than working per se.[7]

Our state and federal governments play a big role in perpetuating a child-care system that is so inadequate. Government standards for child-care quality are far too low. A 1997 study of the quality of regulations governing child-care centers in 50 states and the District of Columbia by Yale University and the Commonwealth Foundation, a New York–based nonprofit organization that funds research in child care, gave *none* of the state regulations a score of good or better. Only one third of the states had minimally acceptable standards, and the standards in two thirds were rated poor.[8]

In recent years, some states have taken steps to increase the quality of care. About 20 states have launched programs that encourage child-care providers to improve facilities and the education and training of their staff. A pioneer in this area has been North Carolina, with its much-imitated T.E.A.C.H. and W.A.G.E.S. programs, which offer college scholarships, bonuses, and higher salaries to child-care providers who get extra training and upgrade their programs.[9]

But other states have reduced their regulation of child-care centers even further. In my neighboring state of Virginia, for example, where regulations were already weak, the board responsible for issuing regulations for the 1,500 centers in the state weakened regulations even more. It raised student-to-teacher ratios in classes for young children and lowered educational requirements for center staff. Now, a director of a child-care center in the state need have only a high-school equivalency diploma![10]

On top of this, many child-care centers in the United States do not have to meet any kind of standards, aside from basic health and safety rules. In some states, religious child-care centers are exempt from licensing, and care in smaller providers' homes is not inspected at all because licensing is not required.

Quality Counts

The relatively small percentage of day care viewed as high quality and relatively weak child-care regulations that are prevalent throughout the country are especially significant in light of the research showing that quality of care is associated with important developmental capacities.

In my view, the NICHD's clearest, most important, least controversial finding is that *quality counts, no matter what the setting.* Whether children are in out-of-home child care or are cared for at home by a parent, it is the quality of the interactions that has a significant influence on children's development.[11]

Interestingly, in these studies, the quality of parental care was more important than the quality of other caregivers' care, suggesting that children are especially responsive to the parent-child relationship, perhaps because they experience it as more intimate, exclusive, and special. This finding about the importance of quality of care across settings of caregivers supports what clinicians who work with infants, young children, and their families have observed for many years—that the interactions between children and their caregivers are enormously important in the development of children's social and emotional capacities, their intelligence, and their language development.

The importance of the quality of care is also indicated by the impact of enriched child care for at-risk children and families. Several long-term studies have shown that the positive effects of high-quality care for this population of children can last well into adulthood.[12]

• A study by Adrian Raine, a neuroscientist at the University of Southern California, found that high-quality preschool programs appear to be associated with positive brain functioning among poor children. Raine's study looked at 200 three-year-olds: 100 were given two years of high-quality schooling, medical care, and healthy food. The other 100 got standard care. He retested the children at the age of 11 and found that those in the enriched program had brain-wave activity associated with greater mental maturity and alertness.

• A wide-ranging review of existing research on child-care quality in the United States found that children who attend higher-quality child-care settings display better cognitive skills, better language skills, and better social skills than those in poor-quality day care. The research found a 50 percent improvement in children's school readiness when they attended high-quality programs with well-trained caregivers.[13]

• Other studies have found a strong link between quality child care and school readiness. A four-university study of more than 800 preschoolers that tracked them from preschool through second grade found that children in higher-quality care were more prepared for school than children in poor-quality care. Children in high-quality care scored better on measures of basic cognitive skills (language, math) and social skills during the period they received child care and on into school. At-risk children are affected more by the child-care experience than other children, the study found.[14]

These studies, along with the NICHD's findings on the importance of quality interactions, send a very important message to families, communities, and policy makers that the environment that children grow up in is just as important as biology or genetics. Mother Nature is not the sole determinant of a child's personality and development. Environment—the communities in which children live, the families that raise them, the government policies that affect them—are critically important to how our children learn to think, communicate, and relate. Consequently, the fact that so much day care is not of high quality deserves our immediate and full attention.

The Effect of the Quantity of Day Care

In addition to the quality of child care, we must also look at the *quantity* of child care. The number of hours that children spend in child care also influences their behavior.

• An NICHD study found that there was a relationship between the number of hours spent in out-of-home care and caregivers' reports of problem behavior. The more hours spent in day care, the greater the incidence of problem behavior. Deborah Vandell reported on this study on behalf of the NICHD Early Childcare Research Network.[15] The analysis showed that children spending 30 or more hours per week in day care were 3.7 points higher on the problem-behavior scale than children spending less than ten hours in day care. In comparison, children in poor-quality maternal care (the lowest third on the parenting scale) were 2.2 points higher on the problem-behavior scale than children in the top parenting group.

The NICHD-sponsored research also looked at the effects of long hours in day care on reports of problem behaviors in comparison with the effects of poverty. The number of problem behaviors reported for children in the poverty group were very similar to children in the 30-plus-hours-of-day-care group settings. Though the problem behavior was not in the range of clinical disorder, the "quantity" effect was 97 percent of the poverty effect. In this study, therefore, long hours in day care were associated with more problem behaviors than poor parenting and with about the *same* number of problem behaviors as the children raised in poverty.

• Another paper by the NICHD Early Child Care Research Network caused a media explosion in early 2001. Entitled "Further Exploration of the Detected Effects of Quantity of Early Child Care on Socioemotional Adjustment,"[16] it reported further analysis of the effects of the amount of time children spent in out-of-home care as well as children's behavior in kindergarten. This paper, presented by Jay Belsky, a professor of psychology at the University of London (Ontario), reported the following: (1) More time spent in care was a predictor of more aggression problems. (2) One year later, when the children are in kindergarten, the greater incidence of problem behaviors such as aggressiveness in relationship to time spent in out-of-home care was present in both caregiver and parent raters. And (3) in addition, more time in care was a predictor of more externalizing of problems and of problems with aggression, a finding that did not emerge when the children were four and a half years old.

• In the case of caregiver reports of externalizing problems at 54 months, children in the full-time group (over 30 hours per week in out-of-home care) were three times more likely than children in the limited-care group to score one or more standard deviations above the mean on externalizing problems. The corresponding rate of increase in likelihood of scoring high on mother reports of externalizing problems in kindergarten was 60 percent and for teacher reports it was just shy of double the rate—an 89 percent increase. It was noted that "more time in care predicted problem behavior in the at-risk range, that is, at levels in excess of one standard deviation of the sample mean." Furthermore, the problem behaviors were clearly more with aggression than with assertiveness. For example, description included "gets into many fights; "bullying or meanness to others"; and "explosive, showing unpredictable behavior."

• Further analysis of the relationship between amount of out-of-home care and problem behavior is planned by the NICHD study group, including a study to see whether it's the same children who at four and a half and later, in kindergarten, show this relationship; and whether parents', caregivers', and teachers' ratings of problems are the same for the same children.

These reports on the relationship between *quantity* of out-of-home care and problem behaviors is of special concern. Data on the beneficial effects of high-quality care, wherever it occurs, cannot offset these worrisome findings because, as indicated earlier, research shows how little care (10 percent or less) is of high quality. These findings on the quantity of care thus suggest that there are a number of features of out-of-home care that require our attention.

• Consistent with this NICHD study on problem behaviors are other NICHD studies on emotional functioning and child care. One found that that "more hours of child care predicted less maternal sensitivity and child engagement."[17]

• A 1997 study showed that infants were less likely to be secure when low maternal sensitivity/responsiveness was combined with poor-quality child care, more than minimal amounts of child care, or more than one child-care arrangement."[18]

• Another NICHD study found that "for children from families at low psychosocial and socio-cultural risk, more extensive child care was associated with more mother-reported behavior problems and lower quality child care was related to more mother-reported behavior problems and more observed non-compliance in the child-care setting."[19]

• Also consistent with this research is a University of Wisconsin study of eight-year-olds from predominantly middle-class homes in Texas that found that children in extensive child care since infancy had poorer relationships with friends and poor work habits and emotional health and were more difficult to discipline. More than any other factor, these children's extensive experience in infant care "was the single best predictor (in a negative direction) of ratings by parents, teachers and peers and of report card grades and standardized test scores," said the study.[20]

• In a study now in progress, Megan Gunnar, a psychologist at the University of Minnesota, who is studying the underlying physiological effects of day care and home care on young children, has found that a full day in group child care (i.e., center-based day care) is associated with a significant increase in cortisol levels in the second half of the day, compared with children of the same age who are cared for in a home setting.[21] Significant rises in cortisol levels are often associated with emotional and social dis-regulation and can be a sign of stress. This effect was particularly strong by the age of 18–24 months. It was present, but less strong, through ages three and four. The differences in cortisol rise between the group setting and the home setting decreased as children moved through the grade-school years.

Most important, the study found that the quality of care is an important contributor to the magnitude of the rise in cortisol levels. The worse the quality of care, the greater the magnitude of the cortisol rise. It appears that the less the caregivers in a large group setting are able to read a toddler's cues sensitively and comfort or modulate his mood and behavior, the greater the rise in cortisol. For toddlers and preschoolers, the home environment and even family-based child-care settings appear to be less challenging than a large-group social setting.

The long-term effects on these rises in cortisol for adaptive or disordered functioning is currently being explored and will be reported in the near future. But this study raises questions about the degree of stress that toddlers and preschoolers experience in all-day group day-care settings and the double challenge it puts on toddler and preschoolers when they're in full-time care and that care is not of high quality.

The potential negative impact on very young children in group child-care settings all day is also highlighted in ongoing research in Israel.[22] Pnina Klein has found that, when engaged in one-on-one interactions, day-care caregivers and mothers with the same child are quite similar in positive caregiving. These include sensitivity to a child's emotional signals, constructive limit setting, creativity, effectiveness in use of toys, and lack of intrusiveness (i.e., respect for the child). However, as soon as the day-care caregiver interacts with the children in a typical day-care group setting (staff-to-child ratio of 1 to 6), there is a "devastating drop" in all these desirable characteristics (i.e., an increase in intrusiveness, insensitivity, etc. on the part of the caregiver). In addition, even when the day-care caregiver shifts to a one-on-one interaction and displays her positive caregiving patterns, the child doesn't express as much emotion with her as with his or her mother.

Taken together, these studies suggest that currently, most of the infants, toddlers, and young children in out-of-home care are not receiving high-quality care. Furthermore, full-time (30 hours a week or more) day care can be associated with problem behaviors and can lead to stress and less sensitive caregiving. In order to meet this challenge, we need to address the hurdles that are obscuring the problem and the needed solutions.

The Social and Political Context

Some of my colleagues have told me they are reluctant to publicly voice their concerns about child care because they fear they will be seen as advocating the return of mothers to full-time home duty. Indeed, the massive publicity that erupted from the Belsky study in Spring 2001, focused on working mothers. But we are doing a disservice to both mothers and fathers and, especially, to their children by lumping the issue of equality of the sexes in with the issue of child care's effect on young children. In turning the child-care issue into a referendum on working mothers, we're ignoring the children. As well, we're ignoring the fact that this is an issue that affects *fathers* just as much as mothers. Shifting priorities so children have a higher priority in the family and in society does not mean restricting one parent to the home during children's growing-up years. Rather, my point is that children's needs must be the chief concern for *both* parents when they make career and financial decisions. I would like to help parents find ways to combine work and family so that children receive the care they need *and* get the experiences they need for healthy development.

Many would also argue the point popularized in the 1990s by Senator Hillary Rodham Clinton, that it "takes a village to raise a child." Nonparental caregivers *can* work with parents as a *team*. But the central question remains: Is each member of the team, and the team as a whole, providing nurturing, sensitive care for the long haul?

Some would also make the point that child care has been around for as long as families. They say that because children have survived thousands of years of being cared for by adults who are not their parents, then there is little chance they will be harmed by child care now. But the modern form of mass commercial day care differs in crucial ways from the types of child-care arrangements that have predominated in the past. For centuries, families worked on their farms or at jobs that were close by. Sometimes they worked right at home. In either case, parents and children were near each other much of their day. Older siblings cared for younger ones. As was pointed out earlier, the nannies and nursemaids who cared for children in wealthier families often remained with the family for many years or even their entire lives.

Naturally, I am generalizing here. Some practices in the past were hard on children, such as the tradition of wet nurses that predominated among the upper class for several hundred years, in which infants were shipped off to the home of a woman who nursed and raised the child until he was returned to his family at about the age of two. Death also frequently disrupted families, and in various eras, physical abuse of children was tolerated, even encouraged.

Many factors lay behind such negative practices, but it must be acknowledged that much of that insensitive treatment of children was a result of ignorance. We cannot plead ignorance now. Now, although we have a better understanding of what types of experiences support healthy development, we are ignoring the evidence.

A Strained System

When institutional day care first began to grow in the 1960s and 1970s, I was hopeful, like many other professionals who worked with children. For families that were struggling, child care looked promising. Day-care centers were to be a place where parents who needed help could get expert guidance in order to improve their parenting skills. Trained providers would care for their children while parents finished school, took a part-time job, or simply learned how to best care for their offspring. Group child care was originally supposed to be for a relatively small number of children whose parents needed a hand with them in order to pull their lives together. Small studies at the time were reassuring. Even since then, a number of long-term studies on enriched day care for children at risk have been encouraging.

By now, however, millions of children have poured into the nation's child-care system. As noted, one half this nation's population of young children—almost 13 million infants, toddlers, and preschoolers—are currently being cared for by a nonfamily member,[23] a percentage that has doubled since 1977.[24] More than half of these children spend 35 hours a week or more in day care. According to a 1995 survey, 44 percent of infants under one year old were in nonparental care that averaged 31 hours a week. For four-to-five-year-olds, the figure was 84 percent, an average of 28 hours per week.[25] My early optimism about child care has faded, and my concern is mounting. The system is straining under the sheer numbers of children who need care while their parents work. It's about time that we questioned our assumptions for the last 25 years concerning the capacity of most out-of-home, nonparental care to provide high-quality care and to facilitate children's emotional and intellectual growth.

What Babies and Children Need

My concerns about the current state of child care in this country are based on years of studying the kinds of experiences that young children need in order to develop a healthy mind. I have outlined them in several earlier books, including *The Growth of the*

Mind, Building Healthy Minds, and *The Irreducible Needs of Children,* written with T. Berry Brazelton, M.D.[26]

These experiences are described in detail in the next chapter. Briefly, babies and young children need

1. Sights, sounds, touches, and other sensations tailored to the baby's unique nervous system in order to foster attention, awareness, learning, language, and self-control.
2. An ongoing, loving, intimate relationship (lasting years, not months) with one or a few caregivers in order to develop caring, empathy, and trust.
3. Interactions with adults made up of long sequences of back-and-forth smiles, voice tone, gestures, sounds, reaching, and the like. These "emotional dialogues" foster the beginnings of purposefulness, a sense of self, and logical communications.
4. Long negotiations with gestures and eventually gestures and words to solve problems, which foster early types of thinking and social skills.
5. Pretend play and spontaneous exchanges of ideas between a caregiver and a child in order to foster language and creativity.
6. Logical use of ideas through a caregiver's eliciting a child's opinion and debates in order to promote logical thinking, planning, and readiness for math and reading.

These experiences hinge on children's emotional interactions with adults in ways that are difficult to provide in most day-care settings, in large groups with overworked and changing caregivers. Families who are capable of providing high-quality, nurturing experiences almost automatically provide children with these experiences. Parents in such families form loving, intimate relationships with their children; they play little games with their babies—tickling them, talking to them, making funny faces at them. They engage in long (several minutes long) "emotional dialogues" with babies and toddlers throughout the day. That is, they communicate with babies and toddlers through facial expressions, voice tone, and gestures. These parents also play pretend with their children: They join in on a teddy bear tea party, for example, or pretend to be a mean monster who catches children and gobbles them all up! They talk to their children in extended conversations about what they like and dislike, asking their children's opinions and debating such issues as whether a child needs to wear a jacket outside or whether she needs to drink her milk! In a family, such warm, intimate relationships last for years.

Of course, no families engage in this way perfectly and many do not provide the high-quality caregiving described above. There are deeply troubled parents out there who simply can't provide their children with any of these experiences. They need the special help a good child-care center can provide. My concern about the extensive use of child care in this country, however, is based on the fact that the vast majority of child-care facilities, whether in a provider's home or at a center, are often simply not set up to provide children with the high quality nurturing experiences that they require.

First, because of the way child care is structured and because of high turnover in the day-care industry, the majority of providers don't get a chance to build long relationships with the children in their care. At most child-care centers, babies change caregivers each year as they move through the toddler and preschool rooms. In centers whose employees receive less training and lower wages and where there is high turnover, caregivers change even more frequently. Indeed, more than 30 percent of child-care center staff changes each year, according to official estimates. And no wonder: Child-care workers earn a median wage of $6.61 an hour,[27] less than the hourly wage earned by parking-lot attendants, and janitors. Few hourly jobs pay less than child-care workers earn.

Children cared for by family day-care providers, who may have several day-care children in their homes, can also experience a high turnover in caregivers because family child-care providers, whose wages are also miserably low, often move in and out of the business as their family circumstances change. This high turnover also creates another problem: Many child-care providers (as a number have told me) "hold back" emotionally because separating from their tiny charges would otherwise be too emotionally wrenching.

In some studies, group day-care settings have been shown to enhance the development of certain motor and cognitive skills. These are important skills, but they shouldn't be confused with the emotional experiences that grow from close interactions and form the basis of emotional growth during the early years. Parents capable of providing high-quality care, and who have only one or two very young children, can often provide these interactions as a matter of course during play times as well as during feeding, bathing, diaper changes, and other everyday activities: They may talk to their infants while carrying them around in baby carriers, while they're riding in the car together, and while making dinner. But because child-care workers in centers are often caring for four or more infants (family providers may have two or three infants and several other children), their interactions with each baby tend to be brief, which means that infants aren't getting the long interactive "dialogues" through words and gestures. Even in good day-care centers, we've seen many an eager, expectant eight-month-old baby give up and stare at the wall as his caregiver stops by his crib briefly but then hurries away to attend to a crying rival. The same goes for even skilled and devoted family day-care providers. They are often caring for several children and just don't get the opportunities to stop and interact with each baby or young child for these stretches of time.

Repeated dozens or hundreds of times over the first months or years of life, these subtle limitations of emotional and gestural cueing are inconsistent with the rich, nuanced emotional interactions that are at the foundation of humans' high mental abilities.

What about relative care? Slightly more than one quarter of preschool children of working parents in the United States are cared for by a relative—often a grandparent, an aunt, or a child's older sibling.[28] Children can reap enormous benefits from such an arrangement because it gives them a connection to their extended family. In fact, for single parents, extended-family members can be a lifesaver. However, the quality of these arrangements varies significantly. If a family member is motivated and is capable of playing a meaningful role in the child's life, then the child-care arrangement can benefit a child immensely. If a relative takes over care of a child reluctantly, the results can be less than satisfactory.

Day-care providers frequently assume that children enjoy a good deal of real intimacy with their parents before and after their hours in the center, and many do. But on weekday mornings and evenings even the most loving parents, busy with work, commutes, meal preparation, and household chores, often find themselves unable to give their children the kind of close attention they would ideally wish. In turn, parents may console themselves with a similar assumption that children are getting lots of these kinds of interactions that their day care! Inadvertently, then, children's need can be overlooked.

Can parents make up for this lack of emotional interaction when they pick up their children and take them home? Can a few hours in the evening make up for limited opportunities for emotional interactions all day long? The honest answer is, nobody knows. Clinical experience, however, would suggest not. The final results of ongoing research into the effects of day care on children may not be in for many years, when infants and children currently in various studies are grown. Although the groundwork for many of our most important emotional capacities—empathy, emotional flexibility, the ability to be a reflective and abstract thinker, the capacity to be a nurturing and supportive parent—is laid in those early childhood years, the results of that groundwork, plus additional experience, often isn't seen until years later.

The question then becomes: How do we protect our children's development in the face of such uncertainty? Most good childcare center directors and well-educated family child-care providers are well aware of the limitations of child care, and the current situation frustrates them as well. Child-care providers are vastly underpaid for the important work that they do. They care for too many children, often under stressful conditions. In fact, given the low status accorded to child-care providers in our society, it's a wonder that all of them don't throw up their hands and go into a different profession.

Why the Controversy over Day Care

In the media and in public policy debates and, therefore, in the information provided to parents, there seems to be a great deal of controversy, and two quite opposite messages emerge:

- Day care is fine for children.
- Day care as practiced is not fine.

The confusion and controversy does not stem from the actual research or clinical observation that many of us are engaged in with regard to child care. The confusion comes from how we selectively look at different findings rather than considering the whole picture. There is a tendency to separate out the real issue of actual quality of care at most day-care centers and day-care homes today, from the *potential* of day care as a setting to provide high-quality care.

As we delve into these important issues, it should be made clear that we are talking about full-day care for infants, toddlers, and preschools. Part-time care may be subject to some of the same concerns, but at a less intense level. It's also important to recognize, as indicated earlier, that *enriched, high-quality* care can be very helpful for at-risk infants (those with worrisome behavior and family lives that are disruptive and sporadic), children, and their families.

First, let's take another quick look at the important findings detailed earlier in this chapter.

1. Only a small percentage (approximately 9 to 15 percent, depending on the study) of out-of-home care for infants and young children is considered to be of high quality.
2. Quality counts. The quality of care, regardless of the setting, is associated with emotional and intellectual development. Definition of high quality includes such important nurturing capacities as sensitivity to the infants' emotional, social, and communicative signals.
3. Long hours in care (more than 30 hours per week) are associated with reports of increased problem behaviors at age four and a half, and all-day care in a group setting is associated with a significant increase in cortisol levels in toddlers and preschoolers, which intensifies as the quality of care diminishes.

The conclusion of these studies is that if a couple, like Melinda and Robert, introduced at the beginning of this chapter, is capable of providing high-quality care themselves, they have to think long and hard about using full-time child care. It is very unlikely they will find high-quality care in most current day-care settings (which are, as we have noted, also poorly regulated).

When we look at the actual quality of child care available in the United States, the findings and conclusions are relatively clear. Why then are there different opinions and controversy about child care? In addition to the political issues discussed earlier, there may be an understandable wish to deny the weaknesses in our child-care system. It's frightening to consider putting our children in any setting that is not of high quality.

The finding that the quality of children's interactions with their caregivers makes a big difference in their emotional and intellectual development can be a double-edged sword. On the one hand, it bolsters those who would like to believe that we can "potentially" provide high-quality day care for infants and preschoolers in any kind of setting—child-care center, family child-care provider, parent, or nanny. On the other hand, those who believe that it is harder to provide high quality in certain types of settings—in commercial day-care centers, for example— use these findings to ask whether small children are best served in such settings today. Which is the more appropriate interpretation of the current knowledge base described above?

The confusion here comes from taking the research on the importance of quality and presenting it out of context. It must be seen together with the studies finding that approximately 85 to 90 percent of out-of-home day care *is not considered to be of high quality*. If we combine the finding that quality counts with the findings of the other studies that the vast majority of day care is not of high quality, we are left with a worrisome picture. Yet many media outlets have cast the NICHD day-care research in overly optimistic terms. One 1997 article headlined "Good Day Care Found to Aid Cognitive Skills of Children" said, "The news about these children [in child care] is reassuring."[29] Another article asserted that the NICHD study "found that children in high quality day care do as well as those who stay at home with their mothers. . . . And in the areas of language and learning skills, kids in first-rate situations do better than those who spend all day with Mom."[30] The text of a front-page story in the *Washington Post* carefully noted that the NICHD study found that "quality of care matters," but the headline cheered: "Day Care Study Offers Reassurance to Working Parents."[31]

Conclusions That Go Beyond Current Research

In some reporting of the NICHD research, the limitations of current research were not attended to and conclusions went beyond the current data. Signal examples of this type of unjustified conclusion based on the NICHD study are statements that "average-quality care is adequate—neither outstanding or terrible."[32]

Such a statement goes beyond what research has shown so far. Let's look again at how the conclusion was arrived at that "average" out-of-home child care in the United States is "adequate"—neither very good nor poor. This conclusion was based on ratings of caregiver-child interactions in the NICHD study. The interactions, as indicated earlier, were rated according to the degree to which they were characterized by positive caregiving:

Positive caregiving very characteristic—9 percent.
Positive caregiving somewhat characteristic—30 percent.
Positive caregiving somewhat uncharacteristic—
    53 percent.
Positive caregiving very uncharacteristic—8 percent.

Are we prepared to characterize settings where positive caregiving is "somewhat characteristic" as "adequate"? Are we even prepared to call settings where positive caregiving is only "somewhat uncharacteristic" as "adequate"?

Do we really know the long-term impact of settings where positive caregiving is somewhat uncharacteristic, which accounts for 53 percent of child care, or settings where positive caregiving is only somewhat characteristic? Do we know the impact of these settings on the most important human capacities for sustaining relationships, intimacy, the ability to be a good parent, hold a job, be a constructive part of a community, and deal with life's expected challenges, disappointments, and expectable range of feelings? Most important, would parents capable of providing high-quality care view such care as "adequate"? Interestingly, while the data exist, there has not yet been an analysis of how much maternal care is of high quality (or lesser quality?). It would appear that putting a value judgment of "adequate" on most of current child care goes beyond what can be inferred from the existing data.[33]

It is also important to acknowledge the understandable limitations in the current research data and research tools. The largest current study is the NICHD project described earlier. But that study population is not a fully representational population (some families chose not to participate).

We also have to recognize the understandable limitations of current research methods. It's difficult at present to sufficiently measure many of the most important emotional capacities, such as the depth of a child's capacity for intimacy, her sense of self, and her future capacities to parent and nurture children as well as pursue a career. In the NICHD study, it has been possible only to scratch the surface, so to speak, and gauge some "measurable" aspects of social competence. Many important social, emotional, and intellectual abilities that are influenced by early experiences are not manifested in early childhood and can't be measured until late childhood, adolescence, or adulthood. These later-developing abilities include the capacity to form an integrated identity, deal with the expectable challenges of sexuality and aggression, and advance to the highest levels of abstract and reflective thinking. Assessing these will require studies that are considerably longer term than the current ones.

It's important to note the tendency to overgeneralize from limited research findings. For example, studies of cognitive language development suggested that these skills did not differ in children in exclusive maternal care from children in child care. The media took earlier reports of this finding as offering "reassurance" to working parents. But the NICHD study also found that social and emotional functioning, which are as important as cognitive functioning, may be more sensitive to limitations in some types of child care.[34]

As we discussed earlier in this chapter, emerging research is raising serious questions about the effects of full-time child care on children's emotional competency. Furthermore, the studies on language and cognitive development compared all types of maternal care, including poor-quality care, to out-of-home day care but did not break down maternal care in terms of quality—i.e., percentage of high, medium, low. It's also important to reemphasize that we must be careful not to draw conclusions about children's long-term development from analysis at age three and four and a half. We need to be modest in what we conclude.

Another limitation on the conclusions that can be drawn from the NICHD research is the fact that it is difficult statistically to compare the influence of certain day-care or family variables and different developmental outcomes when the outcome measures relate to difference developmental realms (i.e., language, emotional, cognitive), and each realm uses many assorted tools with different degrees of sensitivity and measuring systems with different ranges.

The Burden of Proof

This discussion raises a critical question. When dealing with an issue as important as care of our infants and children, where should the burden of proof lie? Should our recommendations be based on proof that day care is healthy for long-term emotional and intellectual competence or is it enough to show that day care is not extremely harmful in the short term? I believe the burden of proof must lie in showing that systems of child care we recommend for millions of children are able to support the highest levels of human development.

We now know with some certainty that quality of early child care counts, and at present, the vast majority of day care does not provide high-quality care. However, when we look at the spin put on the NICHD's reports by some media outlets, it appears that, as a society, we're reluctant to confront these facts. Among the reasons for this may be the sweeping changes to the welfare system in the past few years, which have put a great deal of pressure on researchers and politicians to downplay concern about the quality of child care in this country. A recognition of the quality of most child care in this country would place policy makers in the difficult position of simultaneously requiring former welfare recipients to find child care and get out and work and acknowledging that finding high-quality care is very difficult and that this kind of care is, in any case, too expensive for low-paid workers.

Conclusions

The research findings laid out in this chapter raise serious questions, and the solutions aren't easy. They demand a major rethinking of family life and priorities for many parents. We will discuss these solutions shortly, but first let's state the problem as clearly as possible.

- Early reports that most full-time day care is "adequate" for infants, toddlers and young children are premature and go beyond the data now available.
- According to the most recent national estimates, only 9 to 15 percent of out-of-home care is considered to be of high quality.
- Full-time care—30 or more hours, regardless of quality—is associated with reports of increased problem behaviors. Care in a group setting all day is associated with a significant rise in cortisol levels (a signal of stress), which is intensified as quality of care decreases.
- Caregivers for toddlers and young children in full-time group day-care settings show less sensitive caregiving behaviors in the group settings than when they are engaged in one-on-one interactions.
- Thirty hours or more a week in a group child-care setting, even if it is high-quality care, may not be in the best interests of children in the early years. Clinical observations on the needs of infants and young children are consistent with this body of research.

With these conclusions in hand, what would you tell a couple such as Melinda and Robert, who look forward to being devoted and loving parents and are capable of providing high-quality care themselves? If, in their particular community, as in most, the child-care options appear not to be of high quality, they may have to rethink their plans. If Melinda and Robert are financially able, they should consider structuring their work lives to care for their own baby as much as possible.

In discussions like this, it's critical to distinguish between important theoretical questions and the practical issues for individual families. Families cannot make child-care decisions on the basis of statistical averages, but must base their decisions on the specific question of whether the out-of-home child-care options available to them can compare with what they themselves can offer the child at home. At present, we have to help parents do the best for their children and not confuse an important research question with the practical challenges at hand.

What about the millions of parents who don't have choices? What about parents who must both work full-time in order to give their children the bare essentials? What about parents kicked off welfare who are being required to work and put their children in day care? In Part III, we will discuss the challenge for society as a whole. Providing reasonable choices for all families should be among our highest societal goals. We should not tolerate a situation where families are compelled to put their children in poor care when we know that the quality of that care has a strong influence on the child's intellectual and emotional growth. Child care must no longer be simply a private matter of families, but must be treated as the gravest, most important undertaking of our society.

We need both gender equality *and* the conditions that are best for our children. We need to stop looking at these two issues as being in competition with each other. Many parents are asking the same question—What is best for our baby?—but the answers have not been made clear.

The next chapter will look at the experiences children need at each stage of their growth and development to master their essential intellectual and emotional milestones. From clinical observations of both healthy and disturbed children, as well from numerous research studies, we now have a picture of these experiences. We will look at the milestones in some detail and examine how different child-care settings may affect children's ability to master them.

The Essential Experiences of Early Childhood

A New Understanding

In recent years, research into the development of our minds has yielded some breathtaking insights. We know now, for instance, that young children's brains grow and change dramatically in the early years. We know that early experience to a large extent affects the architecture of children's brains and influences how they acquire intelligence, morality, and a sense of self, our highest human capacities. Early care, it is now clear, can significantly influence how children develop and learn.

Our own research group and other researchers as well have charted the mind's development and mapped out critical experiences that are needed at each stage of development. In fact, we can describe in detail the types of experiences that babies and children need in those first years.

At the core of this early development are emotions and emotional interactions. These serve as the mind's primary architect. Through our research over the years, we've been able to see that emotions play an integral, and perhaps the most crucial, role in shaping the intellect. They play a far more important role than we had thought in many of the mind's most important functions. Even our sense of self and morality originate in our emotional experiences. They make all creative thought possible. The very ability to think and be rational is acquired not through impersonal cognitive experiences but through emotional interactions.

For all children, the most important learning is mediated by the emotions, from learning to say hello to understanding addition and subtraction and even to adopting the proper grammar in order to speak coherently and correctly.[1] This learning, conducted through the prism of personal emotional experiences, continues through the rest of our lives.

An understanding of emotion's crucial role in the development of the mind is of critical importance to parents making decisions about the care of children in the early years. Since we have been able to pinpoint the kinds of emotional nurturing that will propel children toward intellectual and emotional health, parents have a firm basis to evaluate the kind of care their child needs most. Because of the role that child care plays in the development of these critical mind-building experiences, anyone raising children needs an awareness of these milestones.

During the early years of a child's life, nurturing interactions between children and caregivers influence the wiring of the brain and enable children to learn such basic capacities as relating to and trusting others; comprehending sounds, sights, and emotion; and acquiring language, cognitive skills, communication, thinking, and reasoning.

As more and more researchers like me have reached similar conclusions about the crucial role that emotional interactions play in the development of humans' minds, we have grown concerned that this growth is being endangered by poor-quality child care or child care that is not appropriate to the child's age or stage of development, and his or her unique needs. In this chapter I'll take you through the six essential milestones that infants and toddlers move through and show you how healthy families, often without even knowing that they're doing it, help their children through these milestones and how poor-quality child care can interfere with this process. (Interested readers will find these steps described in greater detail in my book, *Building Healthy Minds*.)[2] There are additional emotional milestones that children move through as they grow through the grade-school years and adolescence, but we will focus in this book on the developmental milestones experienced by babies and young children.

Children move through these stages with the help of the adults in their lives—their parents and their caregivers. Whether those caregivers are relatives, day-care-center workers, nannies, or family child-care providers, they play a crucial role in the growth of children's minds. Indeed, if a child is in day care for most of every weekday, day-care providers play a *critical* role in how children negotiate or fail to negotiate these milestones. These steps of development can be mastered in many different ways, and different cultures often have their own unique approaches to help a child learn such core capacities as self-regulation, intimacy, two-way communication, and thinking.

The Six Milestones and the Role of Parents and Caregivers

1. Making Sense of Sensations (birth to 3 Months)

One of the first abilities that all babies need is the capacity to be calm and regulated and at the same time safe, interested, and engaged in their environment. They learn to organize a huge variety of sensations as well as their body's responses to them and also to relate to other people with warmth and pleasure. Once they can do that, they can move on to the next stages.

In the beginning they need sights, sounds, touches, and other sensations tailored to their unique nervous systems in order to foster the awareness, attention, and self-control needed to cope with the new world into which they have suddenly been plunged after nine months in the quiet comfort of the uterus. The ability to organize these sensations, to feel tranquil in spite of them, and to reach out actively for them is the first milestone.

Parents and caregivers are crucial to this process. Soothing, stroking, and rocking the child, talking or singing to him face-to-face, or tickling his tummy lightly are actions that calm him down when he is excited or uncomfortable and help him learn to focus on the outside world. His ability to look outward helps him to regulate his own internal reactions.

Over time, this ability to experience the world as richly and as deeply as possible through one's senses is a foundation for emotional development. The ability to regulate one's internal world is a powerful tool for dealing with the outside world. Every child comprehends and reacts to each type of sensation in a particular and characteristic way. When children develop the ability to regulate themselves emotionally and begin to organize sensations, they can use this skill to gain experiences on which they will build their capacity to learn and their individual identities. Their initial interest in their environment, through a parent and other important caregivers, leads to a growing interest in processing information and people, and in forming those first relationships that are the basis for all emotional learning to come. If a baby feels overwhelmed by the messages he receives through his senses, and tunes them out, a pattern begins that may later rob him of a full range of emotional and learning experiences.

Attentive parents and high-quality child care will create many opportunities for one-on-one interactions that babies need in order to negotiate this first level of emotional development. They will also gear their approach to the baby to his individual nervous system, whether it is highly sensitive or is one that needs extra stimulation. As indicated, babies need *lots and lots* of these face-to-face interactions—gentle rocking, stroking while making funny sounds, and responsive reactions to him when he gazes around this big world into which he has suddenly landed. The majority of child-care settings, however, often simply cannot afford to provide workers with time to help each baby learn to process new sensations and at the same time be calm and regulated. Even when legal standards are followed, and there are only four infants per worker—well, imagine trying to take care of quadruplets alone! Yet that's what we're asking our day-care provider to do. Also consider such physical factors as the noise level in day-care infant rooms, which can be overwhelming to many babies, and the fact that babies often need to adjust to continually changing caregivers because of staff turnover.

2. Intimacy and Relating (3 to 7 months)

This stage actually has its embryonic beginnings at birth, or perhaps even earlier. But it reaches a crescendo when a baby acquires the ability to maintain a level of calm that permits her to pay attention to her surroundings. Then she can notice the tones, expressions, and actions of the people close to her. Before long she reacts to them with pleasure and starts to build intimate relationships with those who love her. I call this the "falling in love" stage because it's when babies develop deep emotional ties with other human beings. Babies begin to learn how to be warm, trusting, and intimate with others by becoming warm, trusting, and intimate with their parents and other special caregivers who are constantly in their world. When these special people look and smile at her and talk to her, the baby begins to smile, open her eyes wide, and focus her attention on them. She studies her parents' faces, cooing and returning their smiles with a special glow of her own.

Out of this first foray into the joys of relating, a baby begins developing a sense of shared humanity that can later blossom into the capacity to feel empathy and love. Without some degree of ecstatic wooing by adults who adore her, a baby may never know the powerful pull of human closeness, never see other people as full human beings like herself, capable of feeling what she feels.

For these capacities to blossom, babies need relationships with parents and day-care staff that have *stability* and *consistency*. The staff turnover in many centers and day-care homes, however, as well as the shifting of babies to different caregivers as they grow, doesn't encourage these relationships to take root. No one would recommend changing a parent each year, but that is what happens when child-care providers change frequently or when children younger than three years old are arbitrarily moved to a different caregiver in a different room because they have reached a certain age. This turnover is tough on caregivers, too. If child-care providers are providing these children with the sense of warm closeness and love that they need at this age, they will probably experience a profound sense of loss when they must move on to other children. Parents or nannies can afford to become emotionally attached and develop a rich relationship with a child. However, economic circumstances often make it rare for families to hire caregivers for lengthy periods of time.

The pace and demands on caregivers in most child-care centers and family providers' homes is also cause for concern. Many child-care providers have told us they have to move around pretty swiftly, even with the most optimal of child-to-caregiver ratios.

When you're responsible for four babies, all of whom are quite vocal about their needs, it can be extremely difficult to have warm wooing sessions with each infant. In fact, our observations in day-care centers reveal that even the most dedicated caregivers have to attend whichever baby is crying and miss many opportunities for deep pleasurable emotional exchanges with the babies who are feeling attentive and calm.

Parents, of course, do what they can to make up for less-than-optimal daytime wooing and intimacy with a great deal of warm intimacy in the evenings. However, many parents are exhausted themselves and have an even busier agenda at home than the child-care providers in the center—shopping, cooking, bathing, feeding the children, and catching up on home finances, telephone calls to relatives, not to mention making some time for their spouses and other children!

Despite these challenges, if parents make time for special play and interaction with their baby after work, it can make a big difference to a child's development. If parents are aware that children may not receive enough of these warm stretches of intimate relating during the day, they can create more such opportunities in the evenings rather than assume that their baby has had her fill of interaction and only needs to be fed, diapered, and readied for bed. Many researchers involved in early-childhood development believe that about 50 to 65 percent of a baby's waking time should be spent in nurturing, loving interactions.

My colleagues and I are often asked about the future development of children who don't get enough intimacy during these early months. Of course, that depends on a lot of factors, many of which cannot be well predicted when a child is young. Also keep in mind that at each of the six stages, including this one, the initiation of a new capacity begins at a certain time in early development, but, obviously, it continues to develop during succeeding stages at the same time that ever newer capacities are being launched. In other words, although we are talking here about the essential care of infants and toddlers, it is *never* too late to engage in warm, intimate times with your child!

3. *Learning to Communicate Without Words (4 to 10 Months)*

This is the stage when the "emotional dialogue" between babies and their parents and main caregivers mentioned in Chapter 2 begins to emerge. Babies can carry on a rich, unspoken dialogue with others through smiles and other facial expressions, sounds, and gestures. These long sequences of interactions can last up to a few minutes each. Dad waggles his ears, baby smiles. Dad tickles baby's tummy with a finger, baby wiggles and giggles. Now he smiles in order to get a smile back. A frown, a smirk, a gurgle, a glance, a giggle each gets the recognition of a gesture in return. Over time, motor gestures gradually become smoother and more polished. They lead to richer and more inventive "dialogues" as the baby learns more expressive and inventive ways of engaging the world. Instead of smiling randomly, he smiles in response to his parents' smiles, or to mimic an adult.

Babies learn that the world is a cause-and-effect world; that their responses lead to reactions on the part of others. This ability to imitate and reciprocate behavior and emotions helps build a child's budding self-definition. The first tiny shoots of a sense of self begin to grow if the child lives in a world that responds to his smiles and gurgles and encourages him to make use of this new power. Over time, the child begins to define that boundary that separates "me" and "you." From these very basic interactions, children begin to understand that their own actions can elicit responses from people separate from themselves. They begin to learn that an outer reality, distinct from themselves, lies beyond their own feelings and desires.

This learning process, however, does not progress sufficiently if young children don't get those long sequences of back-and-forth interactions. The consequences can be seen very clearly and very quickly, even in healthy babies. In one well-known study,[3] mothers of four-month-old babies were asked to give them only blank, expressionless stares instead of the usual smiles, nods, and affectionate coos. The response from the babies was unequivocal. They first smiled, cooed, and reached for their mothers with more and more intensity, as if to say, "Hey, pay attention! I'm talking to you!" When their mothers still responded with expressionless faces, the babies paused momentarily, then tried again more frantically to elicit a response. Within a few minutes they had become irritable and frenetic. Their gestures were disorganized and increasingly purposeless. At last apathy and disinterest set in and they gave up.

If you've ever had to give a speech to an unresponsive audience or talked to someone who stares at you blankly, you may know this feeling of confusion and disorientation. But the effect on babies raised by unresponsive caregivers is infinitely greater, depriving them of the chance to establish effective boundaries for their emerging selves. In the study of four-month-olds, the mothers were able to pick their babies up and give them big hugs and kisses after the experiment. But infants who are constantly deprived of appropriate responses can become more chronically disorganized or withdrawn. They can lose interest in communicating, ultimately growing apathetic and even despondent.

Loving, engaging parents respond to their babies again and again in the course of daily activities, whereas day-care workers or other child-care providers may not have the time or inclination to play lots of one-on-one interactive games with each individual child in their care. They may be warm, nurturing, and loving, but peekaboo games or other games where baby giggles as they tickle his toes and exchange smiles with him may take too long in a busy child-care setting where there is always another child who needs his diaper changed or a pacifier retrieved. Tired or depressed parents will also find it hard to respond to a child in an involved and consistent way.

In the first year of life, babies depend on the adult caregivers to respond to their cues and inspire long chains of back-and-forth interactions. These "circles of communication" are the child's first experience with logic, with the world as a purposeful place. They are important building blocks of a child's capacity for testing reality and eventually being able to understand math, reading, or any one of a number of academic subjects. Without this basic logic, a child won't know how to combine words into sentences or paragraphs or how to stitch paragraphs together into a cohesive essay. Emotional coping—the ability to try three or four ways to get Mommy's attention rather than giving up and crying or biting, throwing, or knocking something off the table—is also first learned during this formative period of two-way communication. Because these important interactions depend on a caregiver who can read a child's cues and inspire further communication, motivated, caring caregivers with time to create these interactive opportunities are essential.

Even in the best day-care centers where the ratio is one caregiver to thee babies, it takes stamina and patience for providers to read and respond to each baby for 15 or 20 minutes at a time. As an example of a positive "circle of communication" with a baby, a child-care provider can do nothing better than to get down on the floor nose-to-nose with a baby and entice him to take the rattle from her hand or play with her necklace or squeeze her nose so that it apparently makes a "toot-toot" sound! But the caregiver will have to be up to these types of interactions with three babies, not one.

Obviously, children learn to talk and think to some degree without optimal amounts of these early interactions. This is not an all-or-nothing phenomenon, except in extreme circumstances, such as in the orphanages of Eastern Europe, where massive deprivations of these interactions have been shown to derail children's language, cognition, and social capacities. Extreme situations aside, if we want each and every child to be as assertive, creative, and logical as possible and to feel that he can use his initiative to cope with and comprehend a complex array of social and emotional situations, it's essential to provide this early foundation as solidly as possible. I realize that in some families, one parent may be better at this than the other. Parents may also respond well or badly on different days, depending on their mood and energy level. Some parents may also enjoy interacting with their young children better at one stage of their development than in another. Some individual families are better at promoting these kinds of interactions with their children than others. Some day-care workers or nannies are also better than others are. But still a general conclusion can be stated: The more children a caregiver must nurture, the more difficult it will be to provide nonverbal dialogues of sufficient quality and quantity.

4. Problem-Solving Interactions (10 to 18 months)

Once a child connects sensation and emotion to intentional action, she can move to the fourth level of development, when increasingly intricate, nonverbal communication equips her to find her way in the world of social interaction and intelligent problem solving. Toddlers learn to engage their parents and caregivers in increasingly long "discussions" without words. These interactions teach children about the pleasure of sustained problem-solving interactions, as well as continuing to foster a sense of the self.

How does that happen? As a toddler advances at this fourth developmental level and becomes able to distinguish facial expressions and body postures, she can now discriminate among basic emotions, distinguishing those that mean safety and comfort from those that mean danger. She has begun to learn patterns in her own and others' behavior. For example, Mommy usually responds when Baby makes friendly requests, but not when she's cranky. Dad loves to roughhouse but not to sing lullabies. She gradually puts together these pieces of herself, like a jigsaw puzzle being fitted together. When a mother smiles at her baby because the baby smiled at her, or when she shakes her head and says, "No, don't do that," the toddler begins to learn things about her mother and about herself. She is someone who can inspire affection and warmth in others. Her mother is someone likely to insist that she do as she says. And so, having earlier blocked out the boundaries between herself and those around her, at 10 to 18 months, the toddler begins to fill in the outlines with some detail.

By 18 months children are often very good readers of nonverbal cues. For example, when Mommy and Daddy come home from work, an 18-month-old will know by their facial expressions or posture whether they are going to get down on the floor and get playful or whether they are going to be stiff and grumpy. Toddlers (as you probably know!) can also communicate quite well without using words. A thirsty toddler may take her father by the hand and bang on the refrigerator door until he opens it so she can point to the juice container. She's showing an amazing ability to organize a complex social, emotional, and behavioral pattern that contains her wishes (the juice), her intentions (taking Dad to the fridge), and even her sense of satisfaction (drinking the juice with great pleasure).

Later on, of course, words enhance this more basic method of communication. But the ability to communicate and understand others' communications through facial expressions, body postures, and gestures comes first and remains a critical skill later in life.

Children who can use and understand nonverbal communication comprehend the fundamentals of human interactions and communication much better than children who can't. They tend to be more cooperative and attentive in preschool and later. They are able to pick up on unspoken cues and figure out situations that might baffle other children. Children who have a hard time with nonverbal communication are likely to have a hard time in school and with friends.

Well before children acquire a sophisticated grasp of spoken language, then, they develop the basic communication skills that will enable them to learn the values, norms, and attitudes of the culture to which their parents and caregivers belong. Toddlers learn to read the unspoken but utterly frank messages of approval, disapproval, joy, anger, fear that the people around them convey. These abilities arise from those long chains of circles of communication, as I call them, that occur with and without words. Babies' exchanges of giggles, grins, and frowns with parents and caregivers gradually turn into long interactive sequences in which "problems" are solved. For example, a baby reaches toward a toy bear. Instead of just handing the bear to the baby, the mother creates a "problem" for the baby to solve by asking, "Do you want the bear?" She is challenging the baby to communicate his desires again, in a new way. The baby solves the problem by reaching for the bear again, this time with a smile. The mother gives him the bear.

Not only do a child's social skills advance at this stage, but also the foundation for a child's intelligence begins to take further shape. The child's mind develops itself to the point where it can see, listen to, and reproduce whole patterns rather than only bits and pieces. For example, a toddler will learn to pick up Daddy's briefcase and stride like Daddy to the door or she'll scold a stuffed animal with the same expression as Mommy when she's angry. Stirring a pot on her toy stove while Mommy stirs a bigger pot, she *is* Mommy. This ability to recognize patterns—which obviously grows more sophisticated as the days, weeks, and months pass—is a foundation for advanced thinking. The more complicated patterns a child can understand, the more complicated problems she can solve and visa versa.

Obviously this stage, too, requires a great volume of interactions with caregivers. At this stage caregivers need to go beyond simply hugging and smiley-face games. Now, in addition to warmth, patience, and time for long back-and-forth dialogues, it's important for caregivers to be willing to challenge children by being a "problem-solving partner." Instead of handing a child a toy when she asks for it, the caregiver may, for example, say: "How are we going to get that?" while pointing to the toy on the shelf and then gesturing to herself or to the child. The caregiver may look over at a nearby chair to see if the child will help her pull the chair over. Then, using gestures and words, they can figure out who will climb up and get the toy, creating a problem-solving negotiation that may involve 10 or 20 circles of communication. This is, obviously, far more challenging than either automatically fetching the toy when asked or ignoring the child's request. But it is an interaction that is far more helpful to the mental development of children who are moving through this fourth stage.

During this stage, children are also beginning to learn how to pick up these problem-solving strategies from peers, even though they are now just beginning to have complex interactions with children their own age. They may follow each other down a slide, or one child may pick up a toy that another child has abandoned, and they may giggle at each other as one puts on a silly hat. But it takes a skilled caregiver to help them learn the true pleasures of interactive problem solving. The caregiver may, for example, show one child how to roll the big ball over to another child. She may ask one child to help another push the truck to a third so she can see it, too. Or a caregiver may be inspiring 18-month-olds to imitate each other in copycat games. For example, she could lead them into taking turns putting on a funny hat and jumping around. If this goes well, children learn to understand interactive patterns and solve playful challenges together. This ability becomes the basis for cooperative play and more complex social relating among peers.

As you may see, the role of the caregiver gradually changes. She or he now needs not only time and patience but also the knowledge to inspire kids to work with her and each other in solving challenges. Parents learn this day by day on the job or from early experience earlier in their lives with small children. To develop these skills and use them with a group of toddlers, a caregiver in a center may need additional training as well as time to work interactively with children this way. There is not a great deal of training in this area for child-care providers. Also, state regulations allow the caregiver-to-child ratios to climb from four babies per caregiver to six or eight toddlers per caregiver. With those ratios, it's difficult enough for caregivers to work one-on-one with individual children and even more difficult to work in groups of two or three. Children at this age are not yet able to interact in a creative, problem-solving pattern in groups of six or eight. Anyone who has attended a birthday party with six or eight toddlers supervised by one overloaded adult knows full well how children at that age interact as a group! Their behavior tends to get either frantic or charged up, or they become more withdrawn and self-absorbed. Yet if you have been present at a birthday party or play group where the toddlers are divided into groups of two or three, each group with an adult, you know that there are marvelous opportunities in a group of that size for shared activities, interactions (two children hamming it up and copying each other, playing silly jumping games, or putting on funny outfits or pots on their heads), and problem solving.

Because this most critical phase of development sets the foundation for the development of complex social and intellectual skills, parents must be concerned with the ratio of caregiver to toddler, and the training of caregivers. If they are unfavorable, as they are in a great many settings, the question of how much time a child should spend in such a center becomes especially acute.

5. Emotional Ideas: Creating Images, Ideas, and Symbols (1½ to 3 Years)

During this as well as the next phase, children's minds make the essential transition to grasping symbolic meaning. That is, they are able to form mental pictures or images—to form ideas about their wants, needs, and other feelings. Instead of taking Daddy by the hand and walking him to the refrigerator and banging on the door for juice, the child can say "Juice now." Instead of just scratching or biting, he can say "Mad!" or "Want hit you!" Children not only experience the emotion, but they are able to experience the *idea* of the emotion, which they can then put into words or into make-believe.

This ability is showing itself when a child loses a favorite toy and says "I feel sad," when she tells Daddy she feels scared rather then shrieking in fear, or asks Mommy to read her a book rather than taking Mommy to the book. The capacity to abstract a feeling and give it a name—to know that a pounding in the chest is fear or that a warm, giddy feeling is happiness—allows a child to bring emotions to a new level of awareness and express them symbolically (through words) rather then by acting them out physically. This ability to verbalize an impulse is the beginning of self-reflection. It opens up a whole new world of opportunities for children. Children can begin to exercise their minds, bodies, and emotions as one. They are able to describe or reflect on what they want rather than simply trying to satisfy what they want. This is not a minor accomplishment. On this small ability—verbalizing impulses instead of acting on impulses—all of human civilization is built.

We see this ability first in pretend play, when dolls hug and teddy bears wave "bye-bye," when toy action figures go to battle or search for a rocket ship. Indeed, the ability to use fantasy and imagination underlies much of creative thought. When children make up a story, figure out how another child might feel, or understand the meaning of a story that Daddy is reading to them, they are making certain creative leaps based on this ability to use their imagination. As you can imagine, the ability to construct this kind of emotional image or idea provides a child with an unusually valuable coping device. When his parents are out and he is with a baby-sitter, he can evoke his warm, loving image of his mother to comfort himself. This capacity takes different forms, each one of which helps us to think.

Readers may wonder why, and how, a child moves from the "doing" phase to the "thinking" phase. Actually, the field of psychology has had the same question. Why does a child stop banging his cup on the table and, instead, ask Mommy for "Juice!" This change comes about because of a critical set of experiences. When a child has a close, warm relationship with an adult, communication becomes important enough to provide satisfaction in itself. Eventually a child's thoughts or images that arise from such communications with a loved adult themselves become imbued with pleasure. In other words, when a young child feels close to an important adult (or adults) in his life and feels understood by those adults, his newfound gift of words becomes very pleasurable in itself, separate from the rewards of ice cream or hugs.

The sheer enjoyment of being listened to, the satisfaction of being understood, motivates a child's first move toward this fifth stage. When a caregiver joins with a child in pretend play and encourages conversations between the two of them as part of a sustained relationship, a child gradually gains more and more satisfaction from the process of communicating, where earlier he needed more concrete things, such as a toy or cuddling. The child learns to appreciate communication for communication's sake, just as two adult friends do when they chat on the telephone. That doesn't mean that the child loses satisfaction in a hug or a wonderful dessert (after all, most adults would find them gratifying as well!). But a child gains a new satisfaction in the pleasures of words. Over time, the word or symbol itself, which represents a concrete need, provides at least partial satisfaction of that underlying need. A child can imagine giving his mommy a hug to sustain him for a few more seconds when he is lonely or scared. He can talk about that wonderful ice cream he is going to have after lunch and almost taste it. Of course, this ability becomes stronger as a child grows, allowing him to be able to be patient and, eventually, to learn sophisticated skills such as anticipation and planning ahead.

At the end of the second year, children's love for their caregivers and the pleasure these caregivers bring them leads children to enjoy communicating in its own right. As a child develops and moves close to age three, caring adults encourage the child to translate his immediate, concrete aims into words and images. These loving caregivers help encourage symbolic interaction by refusing to be intimidated by the child's fierce desires and by helping the child reflect. For example, when a child shouts, "I want to go outside!" a caregiver could respond in two ways. She could simply tell the child that, yes, he could go outside or, no, he could not go outside. This response, however, keeps a child at the level of stating a simple demand. He is not given an opportunity to think about his request and perhaps to mull over just why he wants to do outside.

But a caregiver who asks, "Why do you want to go outside so fast?" is encouraging a child to reflect—that is, to use images to create a picture of his desire. This is what an older child is doing when he becomes angry with a classmate, but instead of hitting him thinks: "Hey, I'm pretty mad at that guy!" Adults use this ability constantly. For example, they can anticipate a business meeting and imagine different debates and dialogues that might arise there. In other words, this capacity is a critical foundation for thoughtful planning and decision-making

This progress from an action mode into a reflective-thinking mode depends on a child's having warm, nurturing relationships with one or a few caregivers where communication is pleasurable enough to satisfy the child's many urgent desires.

As we noted earlier, however, in many child-care settings a sustained relationship with just one or two caregivers is simply not available. Young children are often moved from room to room in a child-care center or they go through a succession of different child-care providers because caregivers quit to take a better job or are promoted. Also, because of the numbers of children, there usually just aren't the opportunities for interactions where caregivers get down, quite literally, on the floor to talk and play with the children (which I call "floor time"). I have enormous respect for the skills many caregivers display when they tackle the complicated challenge of handling six to eight toddlers at one time. How would most parents react if they had to manage two-and-a-half-year-old sextuplets or octuplets, each experiencing some degree of hunger, curiosity, boredom, irritability, excitement, or a bruised knee? It is extremely difficult even for the most gifted caregiver to respond to all of those needs at once, let alone initiate lots of "floor time" with each child. Ideally, a caregiver should get down on the floor with one or, at most, two or three of her charges and help them stage some pretend games, such as a car race or a tea party.

On the surface, it can be easy to brush off concerns about the children's development at this stage because most children in day care clearly appear to develop the ability to use ideas or images and to think. In fact, parents and professionals who work with children often ask me, "Why, if crowded child-care settings are so unbeneficial for children, aren't these abilities more undermined?" The answer is that abilities operate within a huge range.

In other words, the development of cognitive communication abilities is not an all-or-nothing phenomenon. At one end of the scale are people who are more "concrete," that is, they take a more literal view of the world than others. When they feel something, they act on it. A child craves a chocolate bar, so he takes one off a store shelf and eats it without paying. A man's wife angers him, so he lashes out. A coworker's promotion makes a colleague jealous, so she repeats a vicious rumor about her. Such individuals are less able to think through consequences and different scenarios. They grow up to be polarized thinkers with a "my way or the highway" attitude toward life.

People at the other end of the scale are far more able to reflect on their feelings and to delay acting on them. They are able to be patient and work out creative solutions to problems. They are able to sacrifice in the short term for long-term gains. Examples of this kind of thinking would be a child who wants a chocolate bar and asks his mother if he can have one if he is good at the supermarket. Or a man who, when his wife angers him, figures out a nonthreatening way to talk to her about it. A colleague is jealous about a coworker's promotion, so she talks to her boss about what she needs to do to qualify for advancement.

When you look at the disadvantages of being a "concrete" thinker who lacks the emotional flexibility needed to negotiate our complicated world, it's easy to see the importance of getting our preschoolers off to a good start in using ideas creatively. Imagine a world where all adults had a polarized outlook and were unable to defer their impulses, and work out problems and solutions. People who haven't fully mastered this stage of development may equate feelings or thoughts with action: "If I think it, I will do it." In general, I have found that children who have problems controlling their aggression often have difficulty acknowledging feelings to themselves and then expressing the idea of those emotions through words. Instead, they may plunge right into action, discharging their feelings through their motor system—hitting, biting, and pushing. Also, when asked how they feel, if they choose to use words they may answer "I want to hit him" or "I want to hug her" rather than stating feelings, such as "I feel angry" or "I love you." In other words, they think in terms of action rather than feelings.

I often see depression among people who cannot imagine a mental picture to substitute for a palpable presence. People who are able to represent their feelings can use an image of a loved one or of a favorable outcome to comfort themselves when they are in pain and cheer themselves when they are discouraged. They carry within themselves soothing, nurturing images that all will be well, that their efforts will be crowned with success, and that their fears will not come true. Individuals without this inner nurturing presence may be more susceptible to depression when things go wrong.

Although a child's physical makeup will strongly influence his approach to others, to some degree adults determine the themes that children play out in pretend play with other children. For example, if an adult is playing dolls with a child (or is observing two children playing dolls), and the dolls begin to fight, if the adult is uncomfortable with assertiveness and aggression, she may quickly change the theme of the pretend play. But an adult comfortable with these themes may encourage elaboration, essentially saying to the child directly or through their play, "Tell me more about this." Maybe the adult would have one of the dolls say to the other doll, "What made you mad?" That approach is enormously helpful to children. When a child's method of com-

municating his anger and assertiveness (in this case through pretend play) is cut off, the child doesn't just give up those strong
emotions. He simply keeps it at the lower level of action. But
when an adult encourages those themes to develop more fully,
then the child's emotions can be elevated to the world of ideas,
where thoughts and words become the way to express and work
things out.

Similarly, some adults are uncomfortable with intimacy and
may change the subject when the dolls are kissing and hugging or
when the child says, "I love you." Caregivers who are afraid children will become too dependent may comment with a no-nonsense remark such as "Then you have to tie your shoes," or "Clean
up your toys." A caregiver (or parent, of course) who is fortunate
enough not to be locked into playing out only a few rigid emotional themes in her life can help a child experience images of
warmth and dependency, pleasure and sexuality, assertiveness
and curiosity, anger and protest, love, empathy, as well as all the
fears and worries that come inevitably with growing up. Whether
in conversation or in pretend play, these people can often help
children explore and reflect upon a broad variety of these emotional themes that thread their way through our lives.

But here we are talking about the most gifted child-care
providers, whether parents or professionals. It is difficult for any
adult to provide such emotional nourishment if they're caring for
too many children at once. These skills also require emotional
health, intellectual breadth, and maturity. If we're paying our
child-care providers a minimum wage and offering them little or
no training or support, is it reasonable to expect them to continue to develop these capacities? Parents who are drained by
work or loneliness or are under too much stress will also find it
hard to engage in those reflective dialogues. Furthermore, child-
care providers may face special built-in obstacles; many child-care
settings are stressful, harried places where the emotional devel-

opment of children must often take a backseat to the more immediate challenges—getting the children fed, taking them to the potty or changing their diapers, keeping order among a group of feisty toddlers, getting them all out to the playground and back with no bumps or scrapes, getting them down for naps with a minimum of chaos. Such stress or a feeling of being overwhelmed allows little room to listen to individual children, let alone to sustain a conversation.

6. Emotional Thinking (2 ½ to 4 years)

At this stage, children go beyond just having and labeling a wish or a feeling. Now, they gain the ability to *think* with these images. As caregivers respond to children's symbolic "expressions" in both pretend play and in everyday life, children begin to form bridges among their ideas and between their own thoughts and those of others. In other words, they now make connections between all those feelings and thoughts they elevated from the level of behavior to the level of ideas. "I am sad today because you didn't play with me," or "I feel happy because Grandma called." This ability to build bridges between ideas on an emotional level underlies all future logical thought. More abstract logic builds on this fundamental cause-and-effect thinking. This ability to organize thinking is very important when a child enters school and begins to learn basic concepts in arithmetic and reading. "If I take away two apples from four apples, I will have two apples left," or "In the story, Bryan took the thorn out of the dog's paw and the dog was happy and Bryan felt good." Ideas can be linked into sequences of inner images that allow a child to consider actions before carrying them out. Children begin to learn that their actions in the present have implications for the future: "If I'm naughty now, I may get punished later on when Mommy or Daddy comes home from work."

When children have this ability, reason can supplant fear, inhibitions, or obedience. Ideas can link up to emotions: "I'm sad because I can't see Daddy." Time becomes comprehensible, separated into past, present, and future.

These abilities together make up what we sometimes call basic personality or ego functions. Children learn to organize their thoughts, separate reality from fantasy, control their impulses, concentrate, plan actions, and use judgment. These abilities constitute the bedrock of mental health and cognitive achievement. All thought and endeavor ultimately grow out of this ability to create symbols and forge connections among them. A child who is unable to use ideas to get to the emotional roots of a problem may repeatedly and futilely try to force others to behave in the way she desires. When it comes to higher-level academic or social skills, this inability to forge logical bridges between different ideas may leave a child at the mercy of very rigid repetitive ideas or piecemeal thinking that makes their thinking seem disorganized—as though they were always coming from left field. The symptoms of such an underlying vulnerability can turn up in patterns of rigidity, impulsiveness, volatile emotions, and/or poor judgment, undermining both intellectual and emotional competency.

At this stage, children require caregivers who can help them build bridges between their ideas. What's needed are adults committed to having long discussions with children in which children are challenged to be logical. Those discussions can be as simple as engaging a child in a debate about an extra dessert or nap time as well as more complex as an intricate pretend drama with many subplots and character development (where the prince from Jupiter asks the queen from Venus why she loves the man from Mars). In each instance the adult supportively challenges the child to reason and make sense. In addition to engaging children in long logical dialogues, this stage also requires enormous patience, so that the adult isn't tempted into quick yes or no responses and instead helps the child, say, reflect why she wants that game or why she should have all the ice cream and her little brother should have none! This stage also requires that an adult implement limits firmly but warmly, with lots of discussions and explanations as to why the limits are important. The adult helps the child articulate her own view—even if she ultimately can't have her way.

Children at this stage also need adults to help them learn to form friendships with other children so that they can engage in make-believe play together and learn to share and compete over toys. Initially, many children do not find it easy to relate to peers and operate in groups without getting overloaded, impulsive, or stubborn or rigid. Soothing, nurturing adults help children express themselves and, at the same time, help them feel safe, secure, and understood. They help create a setting where children can begin to master peer and group relationships and become another source of growth; this also occurs somewhat even in the stages preceding this one.

As you can see, children at this stage do well when they have relationships with one or a few well-trained, emotionally mature, or intuitively gifted adults. Trying to carry out these types of dialogues, interactions, and group activities with eight or more children is not only difficult, but nearly impossible. Children often wind up fending for themselves or being organized in very structured group activities such as show and tell or circle time or eating rituals so that things don't get out of hand. If an adult walks into a day-care center and stays for a few minutes, it is likely that some children will come running up to make friends quickly as though the adult were a long lost aunt or uncle. There is often a quality of emotional hunger about some of the children, which can lead to a quality of indiscriminateness. They don't seem to take the time to size up this stranger and get to know him. This reaction from children to a stranger is often characteristic of children who are feeling emotionally needy or hungry because they are not getting enough one-on-one interactions. Another pattern seen in a group setting is children playing on their own, somewhat self-absorbed, using either the dolls or toys as their friends. These children may be isolating themselves—sitting in a corner because they don't feel secure enough to deal with the large group of children on their own and feel safer with toys and stuffed animals. Other children seem able to have fun with some friends and size up a new person gradually. It is clear that the opportunities that a child-care center or nursery school provides to make friends, adjust to a group, and try out different activities can be beneficial, but not all children will be able to negotiate this group situation for an entire day. Some combination of one-on-one care and group experience may be ideal at this point.

Here, too, we see a big range of possible outcomes. Most children go on to learn some degree of thinking and connecting ideas and self-reflection. The question is the degree to which they are able to use self-reflection when they're feeling anger or longing. How will they cope with the emotional hunger that they may feel? How many will be locked into polarized thinking rather than taking time to connect and weight various ideas? All we can do when children are young is provide them with the best foundation possible. There will always be stresses and strains that will challenge even well-established abilities. New stages of development will present new opportunities and challenges. The better the foundation, however, the better children can cope with the range of demands that life will place on them. The more children can use those demands as opportunities for growth rather than stumbling blocks leading to more immature thinking and relating, the better off they—and we—will be.

PART TWO

Putting Children First

4

A Parent's Priority

The Dilemma

The dilemma posed by the first three chapters of this book is real and immediate. On the one hand, society now recognizes the need for both men and women to be part of the workforce. In many families, there is not enough income if only one adult works. In single-parent homes, only one adult is available to serve as both parent and provider. On the other hand, relying on the child-care institutions we now have to take over the full daily care of children could endanger the healthy minds of future generations of children and hamper our ability to advance as a culture and a society.

So what's a parent to do? These parallel realities seem impossible to integrate. One reality is what *children* need, and the other reality is what parents—*both* of them—need, as well as economic pressure. In the modern family, both parents have the training, skills, and desire to develop their careers as well as their roles as parents and caregivers. The old assumption, that a woman must give up or postpone her career aspirations and stay home with the children, no longer holds. Yet the specter of women being forced back home from their jobs looms so large over any discussion of the shortcomings of child care that it becomes "politically incorrect" even to raise the problem of children spending too much time in day care and too little time with their parents. Given the long struggle to help men and women achieve equal (or close to equal) career opportunities, that fear is understandable.

The only way we can have a reasonable discussion about children and child care that won't immediately spark a raging inferno of accusations, anger, and alarm is by changing our basic assumption. From now on, when we talk about parents and the limitations of child care, we're going to assume that both parents share in both the roles of caregiving and the development of their careers. They share responsibility for the family finances, the family career aspirations, and the parenting needs of their children. Once we lock in this notion of shared responsibility, hopefully we can have a productive discussion without appearing to threaten the aspirations of women and the much-needed gains they've made so far.

So, if we ask ourselves how we, as parents, can share the breadwinning with each other *as well as* share the caregiving and nurturing that families provide, we can take a fresh look at our dilemma. From this point of view, some solutions start to emerge. In looking at these solutions, readers might also keep two other points in mind: The first is that children can do quite well being cared for by others for a limited number of hours a day. The second is that we are talking about the early years of life, not forever!

A Variety of Solutions

This is where the "Four-Thirds Solution" and other remedies come in. Taken literally, the Four-Thirds Solution means that each parent or caregiver works only two thirds of the time, instead of full time, so that each can devote one third of his or her time during the workweek to the couple's child or children. If each parent worked two-thirds time instead of full-time, a child could receive care from her own parents for two thirds of the workweek.

This time split can sound peculiar at first (especially if you haven't thought about fractions since middle school!), but many parents have worked out something along these lines. Also, I do not mean that the precise mathematical version is the only one. There are *many* solutions with the same effect.

The point of such a solution is to make a practical compromise between child care provided 100 percent by parents and our current state of affairs, where too many parents are spending too much time away from their children. There is a huge difference between a baby or a young child who spends one third of her day (8 A.M. to 11 A.M., perhaps) in child care, and a child who spends all day every day (sometimes as long as 11 or 12 hours) in child care.

At this point, when I'm explaining the Four-Thirds Solution in a speech or presentation to a group of parents, hands start shooting up all over the room. The level of indignation in the room begins to climb. "Am I supposed to quit my job?" . . . "What you're suggesting is totally impractical." . . . "I love my job, I don't even want to give up part of it!". . . "You don't know what it's like in the real world. Good, full-time jobs are hard to find." Even if they're too polite to come right out and tell me their concerns, I can sense it just by looking in their faces.

So let me explain further.

I am using the term "Four-Thirds Solution" as a metaphor for many different arrangements. I do not literally mean that every parent should work two-thirds of a full week. In some families, one parent might work half-time and the other 80 to 90 percent of the time. In another, one parent might work 40 percent of the time and the other parent could work full time. In yet another, one parent doesn't work at all for two or three years, while the other puts in mega-hours.

All these alternatives may be reasonable to particular families, although I'd question the notion that any parent can work mega-hours and still have the time and energy for a warm, intimate relationship with a child. The basic premise of the Four-Thirds Solution is that *children's needs* must be the chief concern in *both* parents' career and financial decisions. Parents can supply the two thirds of direct parental care in many different ways. In subsequent chapters, you'll see how some parents have crafted their version of the Four-Thirds Solution.

What about single parents? Obviously, in families where one parent is a nonpresence in a child's life, leaving the other parent with 100 percent of the responsibilities, including financial support, asking that parent to cut back on work in order to spend more time with their children is not only impractical, it's unthinkable. These days, even one full-time paycheck is often insufficient to support a family, let alone one part-time salary. If a live-in grandmother or other caregiver is available, the child will benefit. If parents are sharing custody, they sometimes can arrange work schedules so that they can each spend one third of their workweek with their children. You'll meet such parents in a later chapter. Often, however, even these options aren't available to single parents or to two-parent families struggling to get by with earnings from low-paying jobs.

For parents in these situations, who are working to put food on the table and keep a roof over their family's heads, simply doing the best they can is sufficient. This is their reality, and I believe that children can sense that. Somehow, as children get older, they can sense this necessity and are more able to appreciate the time that financially strapped parents do spend with them. The fact is, there are many realities that create circumstances in children's lives that are less than we wish for them. But children can sense when we are doing our darnedest to make the best of those realities.

If the reader finds herself or himself in such a situation, try to make good use of the evening hours. (In fact, this advice goes for all parents.) Make your child your companion as you cook dinner and do chores. With televisions and computers turned off, children are often very good helpers in preparing dinner or doing the dishes.

It's a different set of circumstances when children sense that food and shelter are secure and yet parents' time with them is being compromised by their parents' career aspirations or desire for material possessions. In my practice, I see a lot of troubled families where high-powered careers are absorbing much of parents' time and attention and where the pursuit of a fancier lifestyle (a bigger house, a nicer car, expensive vacations, more personal computers, an elaborate wardrobe) has become a high priority. There is a different tone in such families because children can sense that their parents have options, that they don't have to work so hard and be away from home so much. Some parents try to make it up to their children with toys and gadgets and by taking wonderful vacations together a few times a year. But children know what's really going on.

Here, it may sound like I'm condemning all parents who live in big houses or take nice vacations. Some parents can afford these while stilling putting children first. I'm simply pointing out that children can sense whether parents are working to provide the necessities of life or whether they are working to provide much more than the necessities. More parents, in my opinion, could take a hard look at their lifestyle and ask themselves whether they are paying too high a price to maintain an expensive lifestyle. In these cases, I'm not suggesting that parents take a vow of poverty. But giving up some of the power and wealth they have acquired and spending more time with their children will yield a different, yet more precious, kind of wealth. Another thing to keep in mind is that *every little bit helps*. If you can get home from work early one day a week to spend time with your child, then that's better than working late every night. If you're already getting home early one day a week, then sacrificing some errand time on weekends and spending it with your child is even better. And so on.

I know that many parents can't put the Four-Thirds Solution into practice right now because they can't afford it. Even if they are willing to make the financial and time sacrifice, corporate policies often make such flexibility impossible. For this reason, I argue in Part III that parental time to care for children be made a goal of *society*, as least for children in the first three years of life. The healthy development of future minds is just too important.

Even if solutions such as the Four-Thirds Solution are out of reach for many parents, that does not mean that we should just ignore what children need. Ignoring the needs of very young children so some parents won't feel bad isn't the answer. I would argue that parents deserve to know that their children need lots of nurturing interaction with them. First, I think that a lot of parents and caregivers intuitively know this. Only rarely do I encounter a parent or caregiver, including staff members of child-care centers, who tell me that children would be better off spending more time away from their parents. "Parents need to know," one director of a well-regarded child-care center told me recently. "These long work hours aren't good for children."

Of course, there are exceptions to any rule: There are parents who have serious difficulties, such as severe alcoholism or drug abuse, or propensity for violence. In such circumstances, the entire family often benefits from significant child-care help. But I believe that the vast majority of parents are capable of caring for their children in a manner that is healthy and loving. I think most parents would rather think of providing a great deal of nurturing care as a goal to work toward rather than as one to be dismissed because many parents can't achieve it right then. Even single working parents—and that's most single parents—need to know the essential needs of children so they can place their children in the best possible caregiving situation available.

A missing piece of welfare reform that will be up for reauthorization in 2002 is financial support for parents working part-time, and, when needed, education and guidance to parents on child care. As pointed out in Chapter 2, welfare reform resulting in parents on welfare going to work has led to many infants, toddlers, and preschoolers being in poor-quality day care where basic needs are not sufficiently met. Current welfare reform policies are an example of not putting children first.

We must not allow the politics behind child-care issues to distort our understanding of what children need and what most parents wish they could provide. For those who can provide what's needed, this knowledge creates important guidelines. For those who are unable at this time to provide what's needed, such knowledge offers important goals to strive for. It also helps parents make the best use of the time they do have available to spend with their children.

When we think about goals for individuals and society, it is wise to remember that humans and their communities appear to derive their enormous intellectual and social capacities from the long periods of helpless dependency that enables minds to grow and fundamental skills for intimacy, communication, and thinking to advance. Yet our society doesn't fully acknowledge the extent to which children need intimate interaction—lots of it—from those who care for them, nor does it instill in prospective parents a realistic sense that raising children must take priority when they make decisions about careers and work schedules. Our society doesn't tell parents that the most important gift they can give their children is not a good education, elaborate educational toys, or summer camps, but time—*regular, substantial chunks of it*—spent together doing things that are emotionally and developmentally meaningful for the child.

When parents come face-to-face with the reality that children need them and their time, not things, it often conflicts not only with the way they have structured their lives, but also with the years of training they received at school and on the job. Much of a person's early experience—getting through school and establishing a career—teaches that striving for top honors brings copious rewards, whether in the classroom, on the playing field, or in a career. Parents with high aspirations may face a difficult and unfamiliar choice—choosing to achieve less than they might in one area in order to do what needs to be done in another. Those who can combine a serious commitment to intimate family relationships with steady, but patient efforts toward career success can usually provide what their children need for healthy development.

Hard Questions

By now some readers may be seething with questions. Since they can't sit me down and interrogate me, I'll answer some of the most frequent queries I get when I discuss these issues with parents' groups.

The Four-Thirds Solution sounds impressive, but it's completely impractical for the vast majority of parents out there. So why are you even suggesting it?

First, let's talk about vegetables. (Bear with me here!) We know that the ideal diet for children includes lots of fresh vegetables, fruit, dairy products, and relatively few sweets and fat. Indeed, we know exactly how many servings of each kind of food children need in order to grow up physically healthy and strong. We also know that the vast majority of children (and their parents) don't eat this diet.

But just because most children don't eat a healthy diet, does that mean we have to quit talking about it? No! Instead, we teach our children about good eating habits in our schools. We wage huge advertising campaigns to urge children to eat healthily. The backs of cereal boxes feature the "good nutrition pyramid." Parents receive information from their children's pediatricians about encouraging good eating habits in their children. In this case, we don't worry that talking about healthy eating-habits for children will make parents feel guilty. In fact, we try harder.

I would argue that the same is true for the healthy *emotional* development of children. We know that they need lots of warm interactions with their main caregivers (usually parents). We know the particular stages of emotional development through which they pass, and the kinds of interactions they need in order to successfully negotiate those stages. We know that time spent one-on one with their parents is crucial to their development. We know that children need parents there to empathize with their feelings through daily life, to set limits, and to provide guidance based on warmth, firmness, consistency, and love. So why do we hesitate? Why do we tell ourselves that we shouldn't talk about children's emotional needs because it might make parents feel guilty?

Let me say a few kind words about guilt here. We may be so eager to avoid making parents feel more guilty that we sometimes bend over backward to soften our advice. But that's just not helpful to anyone. Feeling guilty is not necessarily bad. It's a socializing influence: It tells us, for example, not to kill or steal, and it helps us remember to "do unto others as we would have them do unto us." Guilt can be a guiding force in our lives. Most of us are parents and most of us probably feel guilty about one thing or another, and maybe this is one area where we should listen to those inner voices! Maybe they're telling us something. Most parents, I'll bet, know instinctively what their children need emotionally. In other words, we can use these feelings constructively to set goals and—at the very least—create caregiving alternatives that give children what they need.

Of course, some parents will throw up their hands and admit defeat, just as some parents have thrown up their hands and given up any attempt to get their child to eat healthily. But hopefully, most will keep trying. We know that every little bit helps. True, many parents may not be able to implement the Four-Thirds Solution today. But they can work toward that goal and, in working toward that goal a little bit at a time, ensure that their child's day care contains the ingredients that children need for a healthy emotional development. This may mean turning down that business trip because it would mean being apart from their child too long or sitting down at the end of a busy day and focusing solely on their child for a half hour. With each such effort, they are creating a better world and a healthier, more productive life for their child.

But doesn't what you are asking for require enormous career sacrifices for many parents?

In some cases, and during certain periods of a parent's life, you're right. Some of the steps I've suggested, and will suggest, in this book entail material and professional sacrifice. But my argument is that children *need* and *deserve* these sacrifices. The plain, unvarnished truth is that parents struggling to raise children in the hectic, pressured world of dual-career couples, unbounded ambition, around-the-clock shift work, and nonexistent extended families often are too busy, tired, or preoccupied to give their children the time and attention that intimate relationships require.

Unfortunately, stepping off this whirling merry-go-round can be extremely difficult. Our culture fosters a desire for achievement and self-fulfillment that resembles greed in its intensity and insatiability. When satisfying all aspects of this hunger proves impossible, as it almost inevitably must, ambitious, well-meaning, conscientious individuals often feel cheated and disappointed.

In my practice, I see many couples who have fallen into this trap. They are enormously successful. They not only have busy careers, but also serve on the boards of corporations and worthwhile charitable organizations. They contribute time to community organizations. But something is missing from their very full lives—a sense of intimacy in the family.

We need to shift our priorities—both as a culture and individually—so that the demanding, but infinitely valuable, task of raising children gets the highest priority among the many conflicting demands made on all of us. Parents and future parents need to plan their careers and lifestyles more carefully so that they can fit in the time and the attention that children need. Just as important, government and corporations need to formulate policies that allow parents to have this essential time with children.

Putting these goals into practice is not easy. Indeed, in our society where many adults are preoccupied with work, adult self-expression, and social status, making time for a rich emotional life and time for warm, nurturing relationship with our children means fighting against conventional wisdom. It can mean asserting an individual set of values in the face of prevailing beliefs.

I'm a single parent and, as far as I can tell, we're left completely out of this equation. How does this apply to me?

When a single parent must work full-time to meet the family's basic needs, the Four-Thirds Solution is not possible. If that's the case, then I encourage single parents to do some creative thinking. Sometimes a grandmother or other caregiver can help and be there to develop another long-term, intimate, nurturing relationship with that child. When I say long-term, I mean that, whenever possible, the same caregiver remains with a child for the first three years or more of a child's life. (There's more on finding the kind of child care that meets these standards later in this section.)

As we discussed in Chapter 2, it's important to realize that the quality of care provided in much of full-time child care available is usually not very high. But, in many situations, parents have no other choice. If you're a parent caught in this bind, then it's important to remember that every little bit helps. Perhaps you can give your child extra "floor time" at the end of a busy day when you and your child have been apart. Set aside a special unstructured time for yourself and your child. During this time, ideally about 30 minutes, you get down on the floor with your child, follow your child's lead, and tune into whatever interests your child. Obviously, with an older child, you might not be literally on the floor. You may be sprawled on a couch or sitting side-by-side on the back step, taking a walk, or sweating it out on the basketball court. The idea behind floor time is to build up a warm, trusting relationship in which shared attention, interaction, and communication are occurring on your child's terms.

Are you proposing that parents keep to this work-family schedule throughout their children's entire lives?

I am talking in this book primarily about the first three years of life. In the third and fourth year, children can do well spending a little more of their time in child care, up to half their day, for example. When kindergarten begins, this may change again.

We can't afford to cut back on work like that. We're struggling to pay the bills each month.

Before giving up, take a long, hard look at your finances. Is that really true? Are there aspects of your lifestyle that could be given up for a few years? Remodeling a house, a new car, or other expenses can often be put off.

We have two low-paying jobs, and we can't just give up a big house and big cars because we don't have a big house and we only have one car that doesn't run very well. What about us?

There are plenty of families in your situation, where parents need to work in order to afford the basics of life—food, shelter, and medical care. Sometimes it's possible for such parents to arrange their work schedules so that one parent is usually home with the children—a "tag-team" parenting approach, and I describe just such an arrangement in Chapter 5.

But when full-time work is essential and you can't arrange work schedules that minimize child care, then you need to fall back on the every-little-bit-helps scenario: Find a warm, consistent caregiver for a child's first three years. Spend time each day in floor time with your child. Squeeze out that little bit of extra time with your child. Make your child a partner with you as you prepare dinner at the end of the day or do the laundry. All of these are small but important steps toward that goal of spending enough time with your child to build a warm, trusting relationship.

What if I can't cut back at work? I'd like to, but my employer won't let me.

Then sit down with your spouse and think long and hard about how you're living your life. Is a different job possible for one of you? Think creatively. Read the remaining chapters in Part Two, where you'll meet parents who have adopted many solutions to this dilemma. Many parents can come up with work-family arrangements that meet the goals of the Four-Thirds Solution. For example, one parent can work part-time for a few years, while the other stays in the workforce full-time. In another household, shift work means there is usually one parent at home. The rapidly developing new technology that allows many of us to work out of our homes in ways never dreamed of by generations of parents even a few years ago is making still other solutions possible.

Aren't you being unrealistic? The vast majority of families don't have the financial resources to adopt such a solution.

Clearly, not all families can afford a pay cut, even for a few years, although I would argue that more parents can adopt at least a portion of this solution than realize it. We need larger societal changes before this will be possible for more parents. We need a culture that regards parenthood not as a private concern and a distraction from work, but as the gravest, most challenging, and most socially useful task an adult can undertake. For the long-term good of each child, and of society as a whole, the demanding project of raising the next generation of adults needs to be recognized not merely as a family's private responsibility, but also as work done for our common benefit.

As I will discuss in Part Three, there is a big role here for government and industry. We need to put the care of children first in our jobs and in the institutions of social welfare. This may mean government incentives, such as tax incentives to employers for providing part-time work options for men and women and more flextime to employees, so parents can arrange more flexible work schedules. Unpaid parental leave should be extended from three months to six months, and whenever possible, parents should be permitted to return to full- or part-time work schedules gradually. Optimally, some of this leave would be paid, as in many European countries.

I have suggested other solutions in Part Three. But the most important point is to emphasize that our children *need* us. Now. We simply can't turn the care of them over to the shaky system of child-care options that we have hurriedly constructed in the last 20 years. Granted, there are dedicated, skilled people who direct programs, work in child-care centers, and run day-care homes. But most out-of-home child care isn't up to the demanding task of providing the truly high-quality care and nourishment our children need for full healthy development. It *is* possible to strike a balance between the career aspirations of parents and the needs of children. We just need help in getting there.

5

Six Families

Trading Places

A few years ago, life was proceeding according to plan for Jack and Gail Beucke. Jack, a bearded fellow with a warm smile and easy manner, was a top salesman at a small software company in the Washington, D.C., area. Gail, a tall, thin woman with an outgoing manner, was home with their newborn son, Adam. She had quit her job as a marketing executive for a national hotel chain in order to stay home with Adam. She planned to remain an at-home mom while the couple had two or three more children, and Jack supported the family. At least, that was the future that Gail and Jack had carefully mapped out.

Then, eight months into Gail's new life as full-time mom, the top executive at her former company called and offered her a plum job—to manage a hotel in downtown Washington that the company had just acquired. The hotel's new owner wanted an aggressive and imaginative manager to overhaul the facility and create a new standard for luxury hotels in the nation's capital. The company wanted Gail.

The job offer was a bolt out of the blue, and it was extremely flattering. But Gail's first impulse was to turn it down.

"I'd love to do it," she told the company executive who called. "But I've made some decisions about my life, and I can't back out of them now. Besides, now I have to consider more than just what I want. I have to think about what's best for our son as well."

The executive urged her to think the offer over before rejecting it.

For days, Gail weighed the prospect in her head. She had thought that once she discussed it with Jack and cuddled Adam a few times, the decision would be a hand's down no. Adam needed her, she believed. Ever since he was born, Gail had sensed that Adam needed a parent who would devote lots of time to him. Adam, blue-eyed, with a thin fuzz of golden hair, was a quiet baby who seemed at times to be curiously uninterested in the rest of the world. He slept 12 to 14 hours at night, nursed easily, didn't fuss much, and appeared content when left alone. He played with his fingers or stared at his Sesame Street mobile as it tinkled and spun above his crib. Gail sometimes grew frustrated as she waved rattles and plush toys in an attempt to coax bright smiles and gurgles from him. Friends told Gail and Jack they had an "easy" baby, but Gail sensed that Adam really needed "wooing" in order to become more interested in the world. The thought of giving up the closeness she'd worked so hard to achieve seemed unthinkable.

To her surprise, though, the prospect of running a legendary hotel in the midst of Washington didn't fade from her mind. In the midst of grocery shopping, picking up Jack's dry cleaning, nursing Adam, and curling up on the floor with him for a little playtime, the offer tugged at her. It was the kind of opportunity that came, quite literally, once in a lifetime, she thought. Meeting world leaders who stayed at the hotel, perhaps even working with the White House to plan important events—the opportunity was a dream come true for someone like Gail, who liked to be busy and to be around people.

Being at home was hard, she acknowledged to herself. At times, Adam barely seemed to acknowledge her presence. The quiet days of her current existence seemed . . . well, boring, after a lifestyle of bustling activity and a hectic pace.

Yet the thought of giving Adam over to a stranger who would care for him while she and Jack were at work just didn't feel right to Gail. Her new job would have long hours, and she couldn't imagine her baby spending 10 hours, or more, each day with a nanny or at a child-care center. It wasn't that Gail had anything against child care. She had plenty of friends who had had children and had quickly returned to work after finding a nanny or a good day-care center for their children. But having children and then returning quickly to work wasn't the life that Gail had ever wanted for herself. She had had a difficult childhood—her parents split in a bitter divorce when she was six, and Gail's mother had had to work long hours as a real estate agent in suburban New Jersey to support Gail and her three siblings. Gail's father, other than providing child support payments, dropped out of his children's lives after the divorce. Gail grew up resolving that she would rear her children in a happy, more settled environment. She threw herself into her career, first managing hotels and then moving into marketing at her company's corporate headquarters, but she firmly believed that when it was time to have children, she would take the old-fashioned approach and leave her career behind for a long while.

Jack also considered himself kind of old-fashioned. He grew up expecting to marry a woman who would, when the time came, stay at home and rear their children. Unlike Gail, Jack recalled being close to his mother. She hadn't returned to work until her children were in high school, and then she worked as a teacher and was always home by 3 P.M.

Jack's father was a more distant figure. While Jack was growing up, John Beucke had been engrossed in his career, first as an Army lieutenant and than as a key aide on the staff of the Joint Chiefs of Staff at the Pentagon.

"Actually, he was a pretty good guy," Jack used to tell Gail. "His interpersonal skills weren't great, but he was fond of us. He was a good basketball player, even though he hated to lose. But he wasn't around much. We just learned to get along without him."

When Gail and Jack met at a mutual friend's house, it was almost literally love at first sight. They were both warm, outgoing people and they "just clicked," Gail told friends. It didn't hurt that they had the same outlook on their future roles as parents. Not that the couple rushed into parenthood. They waited six years, into their mid-30s, before Adam came along. Gail felt she wanted to establish herself in her industry before leaving for a lengthy period, and both Gail and Jack wanted to build up some financial resources before living life in the high-priced 1990s on one income.

Now that they were living out the life they had planned for so long, Gail was surprised that she was considering letting it go. For days, she turned the prestigious job offer over in her mind, searching her soul for clues to the right decision. She asked herself some tough questions: Was she running away because motherhood was more difficult than she'd expected? What if the job turned out to be even more difficult than being a full-time mom? Would she want to turn tail and run back home? Obsessively, she talked to her mother, to friends, to Jack about the offer. Am I giving up, she asked? Am I a bad mother for wanting to work? At home, Gail often dissolved in tears as she rocked her quiet boy as he settled against her chest and fell into a peaceful sleep.

Jack also felt the upheaval. The plans he'd made for his life were dissolving, he thought. Why had the damned company ever called with the offer, he asked himself.

He didn't quite understand his wife's frustration with Adam, he had to admit. He enjoyed spending time with his son. Jack learned to make a game out of catching Adam's attention and coaxing a smile out of him, and he didn't feel as rejected when Adam's eyes seemed to look past him. Jack soon learned that Adam needed as much as 15 minutes before he would become interested in the various rattles and fuzzy animals that Jack waved in front of him.

One day, Jack discovered while playing with Adam that if one of the fuzzy animals "bopped" Jack on the head, and he pretended to be surprised, opening his mouth in a wide O, Adam responded with a throaty chuckle and big grin. So after dinner, Jack and Adam would retire to the family room, where stuffed animals bopped or tickled a surprised daddy, much to the delight of his son, who looked on with interest and gave a wide smile when one of the animals came over and gently tapped him on the head.

One evening, close to the time when Gail had told her former company she'd have a decision for them on the job offer, an idea began to form in her head as she watched the game between father and son. What if Jack stayed home with Adam for a while? At first, the notion seemed too crazy even to contemplate. But the more she thought about it, the better the idea looked to her. Her salary would slightly exceed Jack's current salary, so they wouldn't suffer financially if Jack took her place at home. And Jack seemed born to be a full-time father to Adam. He was more patient than Gail and, Gail had to admit, less apt to take Adam's introverted nature personally.

On day she took a deep breath and sprung the idea on her husband.

"Why don't you stay home with Adam while I go back to work," she suggested at a local restaurant where they were celebrating Jack's first Father's Day as a dad.

Jack grinned absentmindedly as he tickled Adam under the chin.

"I'm not kidding," said Gail. "How about if you stay home with Adam? You know, be an at-home dad for a while."

Jack looked around the bustling restaurant at the smiling mothers, squirming children, and relaxed fathers celebrating dad's day and turned back to Gail.

"You're serious?" he said.

"Why not?" she said. "You can take a couple of years off and spend some real quality time with Adam while I support us for a while. How many fathers get that chance to stay home with their kids?"

Gail's proposal shocked Jack. He realized that it had never occurred to him that the answer to their questions of who should care for Adam could be him. As questions raced through his head, he felt himself gripped by fear: What do I know about taking care of a baby? What would my friends think? What would my boss say? And what about my career? I can't just step out of it for a couple of years to play Mommy. Then an even more dreadful thought occurred to him. What would my father think? Lt. Col. John Beucke would take a decidedly dim view of one of his sons being "Mr. Mom."

Nevertheless, Jack and Gail kept on thinking about Gail's proposal. Gail shared with him the conflicted thoughts and feelings she'd been having. She described her frustrations with Adam and her belief that Jack was the more appropriate parent to be at home with him for at least a couple of years.

"You're *better* with him than I am," Gail said in one of their endless debates. To tell the truth, Gail wasn't comfortable with the emotional closeness she felt to Adam. The overwhelming, scary burst of love, possessiveness, and fear that enveloped her when Adam was born had just about knocked her off her feet. Her own parents had been rather cool and distant. Gail didn't recall either parent ever actually playing with her. She recalled that her mother sometimes sat on the floor of the living room and sang to them. But giggling and waving rattles and playing with dolls? Gail couldn't picture any such thing, and sometimes found herself feeling intensely awkward around Adam. Gurgling and cooing with him felt odd. She felt as if she were exercising muscles she hadn't ever used before. She now realized that she had sort of felt, well, *embarrassed* by it all, stiff and awkward as she raised Adam onto her shoulder and patted and rocked him as he cried. Now she wondered whether some sort of a "mommy gene" had been left out of her genetic makeup.

"Maybe when he's a little older, I'll be able to handle him better. But, for right now, you know how to draw him out, how to play with him, how to make him smile." She swallowed hard as the tears rose up again.

As for Jack, he had to struggle with his dreams of a wife at home and also with his doubt as to whether he could really step into the role.

What if they both worked for a while and put Adam in a day-care center, Jack suggested. But after talking to friends and relatives about the pluses and minuses of the local day-care centers, they decided they didn't want Adam in that kind of environment. Though some friends and relatives spoke warmly of the center, others were less sanguine. What concerned Jack and Gail was Adam's introverted nature. They had done some reading about babies being born with certain inborn physical characteristics, and they sensed that Adam was a rather withdrawn child. They themselves were willing to work hard to engage their son and interest him in the world at large, but they worried that a quiet baby like Adam would get lost in a bustling day-care center or in a busy family child-care provider's home. A well-meaning nanny might decide that Adam really preferred his own company and wouldn't expend the effort needed to draw him out, and Jack and

Gail sensed that Adam really needed to be encouraged to interact with the world at large.

"I hate to say this, but in day care, Adam might just sit there and not get the attention he needs because he wouldn't be demanding like other babies," said Jack. Gail agreed. "He needs to be at home with one of us. And, besides, we've always said we wanted a parent home with our children permanently when they are little."

And so Jack and Gail set out to make the most equitable decision as to who would stay home first.

They sat down and drew up a job description, listing precisely what the stay-at-home parent was expected to do so there wouldn't be any surprises either for the working parent or the one at home. For example, the at-home parent would need to do all the grocery shopping, the laundry, vacuuming, mopping.

"I hate some of this stuff," Jack confessed as he eyed their list.

"I'm not so crazy about it either," Gail countered.

As they debated, despite his fears of turning into "Mr. Mom," Jack found himself drawn to Gail's proposal. Gradually, he began to grow comfortable with the idea. He talked to a couple of trusted friends and was surprised at how nonchalant they were about it.

"You mean your wife's offered to support you for a few years, and you're thinking about saying no?" one asked incredulously.

So Jack took a deep breath and took the plunge. One of the hardest parts was telling his boss.

"I told her I was resigning," Jack told Gail later, "and she shook her head and said, 'Where are you going?'" When I told her I was going to stay home with Adam, she kind of gulped."

Telling his father was not easy. It was clear that John Beucke was disappointed, and puzzled, by Jack's move. There was a long pause on the phone when Jack broke the news.

"It's going to be damned difficult to get another job after staying at home," said his father. Jack sensed a whiff of contempt in the way his father said "staying at home."

Jack shrugged. He'd learned long ago that he wasn't going to please his father all the time. And this was just one of those times.

"Yeah, I know, Dad," he said. "I guess I'll have to just take that risk."

Jack resigned shortly after that discussion, and Gail started her job a few weeks later. Jack plunged into his at-home job. With Adam—now nine months old—in a stroller, on the floor nearby, or in a baby carrier, he shopped, cleaned, and did errands.

Neighbors warned him that the sudden switch from office life to home life could be difficult. Indeed, Jack found the first few months stressful. In the quiet, leafy neighborhood, the midday stillness seemed vast compared to the noisy office life he was accustomed to. He found himself waiting eagerly for the mailman and the UPS truck.

Finally, Jack concluded that he needed to make an excursion somewhere, anywhere, each day. So he began setting up weekly business lunches with former colleagues in order to stay in touch with the workaday world. He held on to his position as executive vice president of the local Chamber of Commerce.

Oh, what the hell, he thought. I'm at at-home dad right now. I might as well not apologize for it. So he took Adam along with him to the lunches and the meetings. It was hard the first time he had to change Adam's diaper in the men's room—especially since it meant changing him on the floor because there usually wasn't a changing table in the men's room—but Jack soon learned to shrug off the puzzled looks of the other men.

When Jack and Adam were out and about during the weekdays, they drew plenty of surprised looks and comments.

"People generally say something like 'Oh, you have the baby today.' There is this perception that it's some kind of fluke," Jack told Gail. "When I tell them that I'm an at-home dad, they're really surprised."

Some even took offense. When Jack was getting a checkup at a new doctor's, the doctor commented on Adam's presence.

"Oh, you have the baby today," he said.

"Actually, I have the baby every day," Jack responded.

"How did that come about?" the doctor asked.

"My wife got a great job offer, and we didn't think day care was the best option for our son."

The doctor threw down his pen.

"I'm sick and tired of people criticizing day care," he snapped. "In today's world, when you have well-educated people who also want children, it's not fair for society to say that one of them should give up their career when they have kids."

Jack was startled by the doctor's strong reaction.

"Society didn't make us do anything," he responded. "We just think it's the best option for our child."

Later, Gail told him to shrug it off. "Nobody can tell us how we should live our lives, and we can't tell anybody else how to live their lives," she said.

Nevertheless, Jack found that he didn't fit into certain aspects of full-time parenting. For example, he was invited by a neighbor to attend an all-moms play group but didn't enjoy the experience.

"I was definitely the outsider," he told a friend later. "Even the woman who brought me said when she dropped me off, 'Well, that didn't go too well,' " he told a friend later. "They were polite to me, but they certainly weren't, 'Hey, come back. It was nice having you.' "

At times, Jack found the long days alone with Adam difficult.

"This is the hardest job I've ever had," he told Gail. "At work, if something gets you down or you just have one of those days when everything seems to be going wrong, you can shut your office door or tell your boss you have an appointment and just disappear for an hour or so. But I can't do that. Adam is always there, and I can't get away from him."

Gail laughed sympathetically. She was having her own difficulties with the role changeover. To her surprise, she missed Adam intensely in those first weeks away from him. The only way to deal with it, she discovered, was to stop thinking about him. For a time, she didn't even dare have pictures of him on her desk because she would get weepy whenever they caught her eye.

Adam, as well, was slow to adjust. At first, when Gail came home from work he ignored her. He would studiously avoid her gaze and crawl rapidly over to his father and hold up his arms to be picked up.

Gail found herself working longer and longer hours. She started early in order to get her administrative work done before heading out into the hotel to deal with the various crises and emergencies that would emerge in the hectic facility. At the end of the day, she had to admit, it was hard to face Adam's rejection. Gail began coming home later and later, until she started missing Adam's bedtime. Jack grew irritated at Gail's long hours. Like other at-home parents, he was ready for a break by dinnertime, and he didn't appreciate waiting as Adam grew cranky or sleepy.

Gail was surprised when Jack finally confronted her. She said that he seemed to have adjusted to his role so completely that she assumed she had carte blanche to work the hours she felt were necessary to manage a job as complex and demanding as hers.

"Besides," she added a little resentfully, "Adam seems to prefer being with you much more than me."

By putting this into words, she began to realize that she was trying to push Adam away because she felt rejected. She sensed he was giving her the "cold shoulder" when she came home, and she found herself believing that this was because Jack was a better parent than she. She became aware that she was running away from feeling hurt.

In the end, the couple came to a compromise. Gail agreed to be home in time for dinner most nights at 7 P.M, and she and Jack agreed that she would devote herself to her family until after Adam went to bed, usually about 9 P.M. and then she could go back to work. Sometimes Gail drove back to the hotel, other times she just did paperwork at home. On Saturdays, Gail took over Adam's care entirely. If she had to be at the hotel on Sunday, she tried to come home early one weekday afternoon.

Hard though it was, Gail worked to connect with Adam. She discovered that he loved rolling cars back and forth, and she learned to hide a car that he, giggling, would then search for. Gail would pretend to be puzzled that the car had "run away," and Adam would bring it back to her as she feigned surprise and pleasure that her little car had come "home."

Jack also made sure he spent time each day devoted solely to his son and not just to errands, chores, and phone calls. They rolled cars back and forth and put together simple puzzles. Adam learned to ask for what he wanted in various ways. He ran to get the crayons and brought them back to Jack, showing Jack that he wanted to color. He wailed furiously at the barber's, but grinned widely as he ate the chocolate ice-cream cone that came after the haircut.

Gradually, as Jack and Gail worked with him, Adam become more animated and interested in the world, although he was still quiet and wary of new faces or new situations.

If Gail came home from work feeling dejected and tired, Adam was often the first one to pick up on it. He often met her at the door with a big knee-high hug and would lead her into the living room. After she plopped down in a chair, he would clamber up on her lap for a long hug.

Jack also began to find other dads who were also at home full- or part-time. He joined an at-home father's group, and soon was exchanging e-mails with men like himself all around the country. He discovered that he wasn't as unique as he had thought: Other men were also taking time from their careers for their children, and they were dealing with some of the same issues—the wariness they faced from at-home moms, the jokes about "Mr. Mom," and the polite scrutiny they encountered from postal carriers, super-market clerks, and schoolteachers.

"Everyone assumes I'm out of a job and lying on the couch watching ESPN all day while the kids run wild," confided one at-home dad in the at-home dad's on-line chat-room discussion that Jack participated in. Jack smiled in recognition when he read that on his home computer. How familiar it sounded!

Over time, as Jack settled into his role, he was able to offer comfort and some encouraging words to the "newbie" at-home fathers. Have a sense of humor, he urged them. Think about how lucky you are to spend all this time with your kids. What about the fathers who were putting in 90-hour workweeks?

At times, though, Jack's remaining doubts spilled over into other areas of his relationship with Gail. For a time, he felt uneasy about pursuing sex and intimacy with Gail. He had always taken the initiative in the romantic part of their lives. But with his changed career role, he often found himself thinking that she would meet more exciting men at work and that she wouldn't desire him as much. He lost his confidence and stopped pursuing her.

Gail mistakenly assumed Jack was either angry or jealous or that she was no longer attractive to him because she was too "masculine." Fortunately, after a few months of little to no sexual activity, Gail became angry with Jack and accused him of no longer loving her. This dramatic statement really shook up Jack, but it also let him know that his assumption that Gail was no longer interested in him sexually was incorrect. It led to a series of confessions by both of them about their worries over the last few months. They decided to get a sitter on Friday or Saturday nights, and make time for each other—for talking, being together, and sharing the intimacies that they had enjoyed during their courtship days.

Gail became pregnant again when Adam was two years old, and now a new set of decisions arose. They debated who would stay home next. Those weren't easy discussions. Jack had always assumed that he would head back into the workplace and that Gail would take over. But Gail surprised even herself by saying that she wanted to take a brief maternity leave and then head back to work.

At first, Jack wasn't happy. He hadn't seen his stint at home as a long-term commitment. He felt panicked about his future employability. As Gail's pregnancy progressed, Jack went out on some job interviews. It was difficult. Many potential employers raised their eyebrows at his explanation of the two-year gap on his résumé, which infuriated Jack. One executive told Jack he was concerned about Jack's "commitment" to a job. Although he didn't refer specifically to Jack's time as an at-home dad, Jack knew that was what he meant.

"So this is what women go through when they try to get back to work after staying home with the kids," he said dryly to Gail. She smiled, hoping, quite frankly, that Jack would just give it up and accept that he was a more gifted parent than she.

"Well," said Gail, "In their eyes, I guess, you *have* done something wrong. You put your family before a job, and a lot of people have a problem with that."

In the end, the couple struck a compromise. Jack continued to stay at home, but he began to build a small consulting business based on his technological skills and his knowledge of the

Internet. They built a small office for Jack in the basement of their home, and he retreated there when Adam, now two, went to a small play group for a few hours and during some evenings and weekends.

This new arrangement meant that Jack got less done around the house, which was hard for Gail. She'd gotten used to coming home to a relatively neat house and a hot meal at the end of the day.

Another compromise had to be struck. With the extra cash that Jack was bringing in, they hired a housekeeper to come once a week to clean, do some grocery shopping, and get the laundry going. Both Jack and Gail, a fairly frugal pair, disliked spending the extra money, but they agreed that it was best in order to preserve the harmony of the family.

When Elizabeth was born, Gail took a three-month maternity leave, while Jack built his consulting business. When the three months was over, Gail went back to work, and Jack stayed home with Elizabeth and Jack.

None of this was an easy experience for either Gail or Jack. Gail suffered plenty of pangs of guilt at leaving her children behind at home, although she was now able to keep photos of her children on her desk at work. She felt guilty for working so much. She also had painful feelings about sometimes being No. 2 in her children's eyes.

Jack struggled to keep his consulting business going at home and finally realized that it was only going to be a minor part of his life until the children were older. Adam had already begun preschool, so he could see light at the end of the tunnel. He continued to stay active in the local Chamber of Commerce and stayed in touch with former colleagues. "I'll be back there someday," he told Gail. "I may need them!"

Jack also developed a thicker skin about his "Mr. Mom" role, learning to brush off the occasional comments and surprised looks. At Adam's three-morning-a-week nursery school, he would proudly tell his classmates, "My daddy stays with me. My mommy goes to a office."

Gail and Jack's story shows the positive changes that can result when a couple is able to adapt to changing circumstances. It's often hard for couples to anticipate where new experiences can lead. Gail hadn't anticipated that she would want to continue working even when her second child was born, and Jack would have been shocked to learn that he'd end up being the stay-at-home dad for two children. Yet over time, both parents relaxed more into their acquired roles, and each one recognized, although it was unspoken, that each was doing what felt most natural. Jack felt relaxed at home with the kids, and Gail found herself more relaxed in the structure of the workplace.

Wooing and nurturing children did not come naturally to Gail, and she had to work hard at it—especially when she had had a busy day at work—and the children reacted by giving her the cold shoulder at home. Many moms and dads who work face her challenge. Sometimes a child may try to distance herself from the parent who works. Mothers whose husbands are picking up the lion's share of the child-care time are discovering how hard it is to be replaced as the primary object of the child's love.

Gail's initial reaction to pull away is fairly common. When a child appears aloof or distant, a natural reaction is to want to retreat from that child a bit. Parents may rationalize this apparent indifference from their child as a sign that a he is "growing up and doesn't need me as much." Or they may decide that their children really prefer their spouses to them. Many fathers have worked longer and longer hours, rationalizing that they aren't really needed at home.

Gail was tempted to adopt just that approach and to let Jack take over. But instead of pulling away, parents need to take the opposite approach. They need to woo their children back. They need to be playful and spend time when they arrive home in the evening to connecting again with their children. It's very easy to become defensive about children who appear aloof or distant and to pull away yourself. But if you pull away often enough, it can place a permanent impediment on your relationship with your children. A better approach is to bring back the warmth and intimacy in your relationship with your child. Gail, for example, had to learn to be patient as she coaxed the children into a game or tickled their tummies until they had to laugh in spite of themselves.

Parents may worry that they don't know how to do this. They have plenty of company! Many parents find the more emotional aspects of parenting a challenge. That's because parenting is an acquired skill, not something we were born with. If we had parents who, for whatever reasons, weren't nurturing and warm, then we often have to struggle to develop those qualities as parents ourselves. But never stop trying. Remind yourself that the way to learn to be a parent is to parent. No one can hand you a book guaranteed to turn you into the world's perfect parent. It's on-the-job training from the moment of birth. But you have to be in the trenches to learn how to do it! If you're not in the trenches, you can't learn.

It helps to see parenting as a career. Like all careers, you struggle your way up the ladder. You're not born with the skills to be a good, say, manager or accountant. As you proceed, you make mistakes and learn from them, and you repeat the process as you go. None of us (not even child psychiatrists!) gets it right all the time with our own children. But parents have 20 years, more or less, to keep trying.

Jack had to work on a different dilemma. He was satisfying many of his nurturing desires, which many fathers never get a chance to fully explore. But he also had a strong desire to build a successful career and to fulfill all the expectations of success instilled in him by his strong father, even though he resented his father's controlling voice. Practically speaking, however, it isn't easy for anyone to keep his eye on future career prospects amid at-home parenting chores. More than once, Jack found himself wanting to escape into the luxury of simply being the best at-home parent in the country. He recognized that at times he was carrying on a silent argument with his father, in which his father accused him of "hiding out." But Jack knew in his heart that life wasn't that simple. He probably was not going to fully resolve his internal battle. He recognized that he would simply have to strug-gle with both inclinations—to do best by the children and to keep up his business contacts and consulting for the foreseeable future. Jack has stayed committed to being at home with the chil-dren, until they are in grade school.

As for Jack and Gail's sex life, Jack's assumption that Gail was meeting more exciting men at work, and Gail's assumption that Jack was less interested in her sexually, are misunderstandings that are fairly common, regardless of who is at home and who is out in the world. Insecurities quickly give rise to fantasies that can be difficult to correct. Many couples aren't as fortunate as Jack and Gail. They continue to misperceive each other's intentions, which can lead to ongoing difficulties around intimacy. The way out of this jam is honest and open discussion of each other's thoughts and assumptions about each other sexually. Often, the desire for emotional and sexual intimacy is as strong as ever.

Tag-Team Parents

Athelia Johnston grabbed the dish towel and took a swipe at her eldest daughter.

"Watch out!" she said.

Twelve-year-old Alicia just laughed and danced out of her mother's way. She knew when her mom was joking, and judging by the twinkle in her mother's eyes, this was one of those times.

"Momma!" she yelled, her eyes dancing also. "I don't want to do my homework. And you can't make me!"

Athelia laughed and gave her daughter a quick hug. "Oh, yes I can. But you're smart enough to know that. So get to those books and show those teachers how smart you are."

It was the end of a long day, Athelia thought, as she drew a long, deep breath. But then, all her days were long right now. After getting off work at 3 P.M. from her job as a high school secretary, she raced home so that Derek could head out to his job as a police officer. They didn't have much time for anything more than a quick kiss at the door when she dashed in at 3:45. Derek's shift started at 4:30, and he couldn't be sure how the drive was going to be. The "kid hand-off" as they liked to call it, hadn't gone smoothly that day. One-year-old Derek Jr. wailed furiously as his dad deposited him on the floor so he could pull on his coat and retrieve his gun from the small locked cabinet on the top shelf of the hall closet. Just then, three-year-old Monique tried to wrestle one of Derek Jr.'s cars away from him, which didn't help matters—especially when Monique gave up on the car and smacked Derek on the head. Derek Jr. screeched while Monique launched into a full-scale temper tantrum, kicking and screaming, as she lay on the floor. "Derek won't give me the car!" she howled. "I want the car!"

It wasn't until hours later—when Derek arrived home just as Athelia was falling asleep and told her that Derek Jr. and Monique had been battling over the car all afternoon—that Athelia learned just what had sparked the imbroglio.

"I wish you'd told me what a mess I was walking into," Athelia murmured as she set her alarm for 5:30 in the morning.

"No time, baby," said Derek with a tired sigh. "No time."

And so it was in the Johnston household. Tag-team, they called it.

"Tag, you're it," Derek would say jokingly when he handed over Derek Jr. as he headed out the door.

"Tag, you're it," Athelia would mouth silently as she crept in to check on her sleeping children before slipping out of the house for work at 6:15 in the morning, hoping that Derek Jr. would stay asleep this time so his dad could slumber for a while longer. Sometimes Alicia got up with Derek Jr. if he woke up, but Athelia knew that it was hard on her oldest daughter.

Despite the chaos and the constant fatigue they felt, Athelia and Derek felt they wouldn't have had it any other way. They'd carefully planned their lives to try to incorporate family and work in a way that wouldn't shortchange any of it.

This was a second marriage for Athelia, a first for Derek. They had met about four years ago through friends. Athelia was struggling to cope with being single after her husband abruptly walked out on her and Alicia, who was three at the time. Athelia hadn't been looking for another relationship—let alone marriage—when Derek had suddenly appeared. Alicia was still in anguish over her parents' breakup and not willing to embrace this stranger.

But in the end, Athelia and Derek decided they had too much of a good thing going and were married. The decision to have more children was tougher on Athelia than it was on Derek. Athelia, then 28, wanted to wait to settle into this sudden transformation of her life, but Derek, 32, was eager to start a family. He'd spent some time in the Army after graduating from high school, then had joined the police force in the small Arizona city where he grew up.

Athelia had married her high school boyfriend after graduation and had gotten a job with the school system. Until Alicia was born, Athelia was going to school at night to earn her college degree. Her husband worked as a computer programmer at a local high-tech company. Then followed the "hard years," as Athelia called them. Her husband ended their marriage. Athelia abandoned her college studies and scrambled for a better-paying job on which to support Alicia and herself. Arranging baby-sitting for Alicia was a mad scramble. Sometimes her mother and sisters watched Alicia, sometimes Athelia relied on neighbors. Her ex-husband was supportive, but he was laid off just as they were divorced, and he fell into a depression and was unable to find steady work for several years. He visited Alicia frequently, but there was a time when Athelia couldn't count on him financially until he got back on his feet.

When Athelia and Derek married, they agreed that these haphazard child-care arrangements had to stop. Athelia considered quitting her job, but a junior police officer's salary just wasn't enough to live on in their community. Besides, said Athelia, very few women she knew were stay-at-home moms. Black women had always worked outside the home. Her grandmother had had five children and had barely missed a day of work. It didn't feel right to her to place the burden of providing for the family solely on Derek's shoulders.

In the end it was Derek who came up with the solution to their child-care dilemma. He volunteered to work the evening shift at work: 4:30 P.M. to 12:30 A.M., so he would be home during the day until Athelia came home from school.

The arrangement worked well. Alicia seemed much happier.

Monique was born three years ago, and Derek Jr. came along a year ago, and then, as Derek Sr. liked to say, "things got really crazy." Again, they revisited the idea of having Athelia quit her job and stay home, but it just wasn't financially feasible. So they stayed with the arrangement that had worked—tag-team parenting. Their families offered to help them out when they could and, it came in handy when Derek had to make a court appearance for his job during the day when Athelia was at work.

When things got really hectic, Athelia leaned on her church, which had sustained her through all those lean years. She sang in the choir, which practiced once a week, and she looked forward with anticipation each week to that hour that was "just for me," she said.

At times, the pace of their life left her breathless. "Sometimes I think it was easier when it was just Alicia and I," Athelia groaned to a friend. "Now it's three kids, two jobs, and nothing's getting done. The laundry just sits there. Derek and I play this game where we wait to see who gets sick of dirty clothes first. Whoever does, they kind of give in and start washing clothes. At least when it was Alicia and I, we had clean clothes most of the time. We didn't have a lot of underwear, but it was clean!" Athelia laughed, but she didn't feel very cheerful. She had always enjoyed cooking, but now she relied on fast food and frozen food.

It feels like a part of me is dying, she thought wistfully.

Derek, too, felt a sense of loss. He mourned the days when he could swing by and pick Alicia up from school, and they would stop for a soda before he dropped her off at home and headed into work. Now, he scrambled to get Derek Jr. and Monique looking pretty good before Athelia flew in the door.

The children, however, thrived on the continual attention from both parents. The strain on Derek and Athelia wasn't evident to them. Alicia loved coming home from school, instead of taking the bus to her day-care center. She would drop her books on the floor just inside the kitchen door and talk to her mom while she had a snack and Derek Jr. and Monique fought to climb onto her lap. At times, she thought, it was hard to share her mom with her half brother and half sister, but she could live with that.

Derek Jr. and Monique were quite a pair. Of the two, Monique was the most outgoing. She loved pulling mischievous tricks like hiding in the mountain of laundry that towered over her in the basement and popping out and yelling, "Boo!" when her mom came downstairs looking for her. Monique would fall over from laughing if she startled her mom enough to make her jump. A small girl with lively black eyes and a thin face, she was constantly pulling stunts like that.

Derek was the quieter of the two children. He enjoyed watching his big sister pester his parents and Alicia. Blessed with a sweet personality and a wide, warm smile, he nevertheless held his own with his more outgoing sister. He howled furiously if she stole his "Blankie," the blue-and-white blanket that he carried constantly, and squealed if she stole his favorite truck while he was playing with it.

Their parents, however, felt like they were whirling through the house on the edge of a tornado. Derek worked weekend evenings, and since his days off—Monday and Tuesday—were often taken up with court appearances, the family was rarely together. Saturday mornings were reserved for chore time, and Sunday mornings were for church.

As the time passed, Derek and Athelia found themselves becoming increasingly irritated with each other. Athelia grew more irritated with Derek for the household chores that went undone in the mornings when she was at work. She hated coming home in the afternoons to dirty breakfast dishes still in the sink and unmade beds, but it happened often. Athelia who really liked being organized in her life, couldn't stand the mess. She tried leaving Derek polite notes— "Please put dishes in dishwasher!!!!" and "Make beds!!!!" but it did no good.

Derek was also bothered by the mess. But he had to prioritize, and he felt that activities like taking Derek Jr. and Monique to the library or to the park took priority over cleaning up the mess.

Athelia felt she was being left with full responsibility for the house. When her notes were ignored, she escalated the situation by nagging at Derek. She would phone him from work to remind him to clean the bathroom or put some potatoes on to boil.

Derek tried to keep up, but, as for Athelia, there was just too much for the both of them to do each day.

As the tensions mounted, with Athelia and Derek each assuming the other wasn't carrying enough of the load, Athelia and Derek's sex life tapered off. Derek began spending more time at work late at night, while Athelia stewed at home. When they were together and home, Athelia found herself snapping at Derek for the tiniest things—how he answered the telephone, how he fed Derek Jr. his meals, even how he changed lightbulbs! As her anger festered, she began clamping down harder. Derek responded by growing more and more silent. Whenever Athelia nagged, his face grew taut and his lips tightened. He would finish whatever he was doing and then silently retreat to the garage or head out to the hardware store.

The children reacted differently to this growing tension. Derek Jr., who had been sleeping 12 hours at night, started waking up more often, and it was hard to settle him down. He also seemed more irritable and became more easily frustrated during the day when he couldn't get what he wanted. Monique started developing fears that she hadn't had before. She wouldn't go upstairs unless someone else came with her, and she screamed hysterically if Athelia or Alicia left her alone—especially upstairs. She was even a bit more hesitant to play at friends' houses than she used to be.

The quality of playtime also deteriorated in the household as Derek and Athelia became more preoccupied with the growing tension between them. Their tag-team schedule, while challenging, had left them with more opportunities for one-on-time time with their children than many dual-career couples had. They used to have what they called "fun time" with their children—especially Derek Jr. and Monique. They could get Derek Jr. laughing and giggling by pretending to be a little doggie and running away while Derek Jr. toddled after them. "Fun time" with Monique was when one of her parents pretended to be the beast in "Beauty and the Beast," one of Monique's favorite stories, while Monique pretended to be Belle.

But both Derek and Athelia found themselves withdrawing from this play time. With the growing tension, Athelia and Derek tended to turn on the television more often to keep the kids busy, and they let Derek Jr. and Monique play with each other more. Soon, their play became less imaginative than it had been before. Instead of being rich and varied, the children's play became more self-absorbed and mechanical: moving cars back and forth or simply banging on their toys.

Alicia started telling her friends' parents that her mom and stepdad were getting divorced, even though there had been no mention of this in the household. Athelia only found out about it when the parent of one of Alicia's friends inquired about the pending "divorce" and asked whether there was anything she could do! Athelia was horrified and couldn't imagine why Alicia would be "making up stories." But it was clear that Alicia, given her earlier experience, was getting nervous about the bickering and the tension.

It took a crisis to pull Derek and Athelia back together. One night after dinner, Derek Jr. began crying softly. Athelia could see blotches growing on his face and neck. His breathing grew ragged and hoarse.

Athelia grabbed her son out of his high chair and fought down panic, her thoughts torn and jumbled. *What do I do now?* She thought for a moment. As Derek's breathing grew more hoarse, Monique sensed that something was wrong and began screaming. The sound of Monique's voice shook Athelia out of her shocked state, and she shifted into action.

"It's all right, sweetheart," she said quietly, grabbing for the phone and dialing 911. In a split second, her call was answered.

"My son . . . can't breathe," she said urgently, cradling Derek Jr. against her. Monique dove across the room and wrapped herself around Athelia's legs, still wailing. As she hung up the phone, Athelia shouted for Alicia.

"Take Monique!" she ordered as Alicia appeared in the doorway, looking astonished at the turbulent scene in front of her. "Derek can't breathe."

As Alicia grabbed for Monique, Athelia lay Derek on the floor. His eyes were beginning to close and his breath was growing fainter, his skin turning pale. Oh, God, dear God, help us she prayed silently as she tried to recall details from the CPR course she'd taken last year. She tilted her son's head back and fitted her mouth over his. *Breathe . . . 1, 2, 3. . . . Breathe in . . . 1, 2, 3 . . . Oh God, I hope this is right . . . Breathe 1, 2, 3 . . . Derek, my baby, my love, take a breath. . . .* Far off somewhere, she heard the wailing of a siren until it stopped abruptly, and suddenly two paramedics were leaning over her. Now the crackle of their two-way radios filled the room as they worked quickly and efficiently over her son.

Athelia shouted up the stairs to Alicia, telling her to call Derek and tell him to meet them at the hospital. In the ambulance, she huddled in the corner, praying with all her might as she strained to catch glimpses of her son as the paramedics tended to him. Then she was in the waiting room of the emergency room, where Derek found her and wrapped his arms around her. She felt suddenly breathless and pressed herself against his uniform, still chilly from the winter air outside. She could feel his heart thudding against her cheek as they huddled together. "He couldn't breathe," she said. There didn't seem much reason to say anything else.

After a tense hour, Derek and Athelia were called back to the curtained-off area where they had taken Derek. A doctor took Athelia by the elbow and steered her toward a crib. Derek Jr.'s eyes were closed, and he wore an oxygen mask. He was breathing.

"You're his parents?" the doctor asked gently. Derek and Athelia both nodded.

"Your son, it appears, had an allergic reaction to something. We don't know what yet," the doctor continued. "Does he have any severe allergies?"

Derek and Athelia looked at each other and then shook their heads at the doctor. Athelia still didn't trust herself to speak, but Derek cleared his throat.

"Not that we know of," he told the doctor.

"Well, we'll need to figure out what happened," she said, but added with a tired smile. "But your son is on the mend."

Athelia sagged against Derek as he clutched her, both of then weeping.

It turned out to be fairly easy to figure out what had triggered Derek Jr.'s allergic reaction. Athelia and Derek went through everything he had eaten that day.

"Anything new? Anything different?" the doctor asked. Athelia started to shake her head and then stopped with a gasp. Alicia had brought a bag of peanuts home from school, and the little boy had been entranced by the nuts in their bumpy brown shells. Athelia had permitted Derek to have a few after dinner under her close supervision. It was after that that Derek's breathing difficulties started.

The doctor nodded. "I can't say for sure, but it sounds like your little boy may have a severe allergy to peanuts. We're seeing more children with allergies to peanuts or nuts in general. Has he had them before?"

Athelia thought for a moment. "I don't think so. I don't like peanuts, so I don't even keep peanut butter around."

With that, Athelia and Derek embarked on a journey to heal their son—and their marriage. Derek Jr., it turned out, did indeed have a deadly allergy to nuts. Even one small bite could send him into anaphylactic shock, causing his throat to swell. The end result, unless he received prompt medical attention, could be death.

After a few days in the hospital, Derek Jr. came home as his sweet, eager self, but Athelia and Derek realized how close they'd come to losing him. They rid the house of any nuts they could find and equipped themselves with an EpiPen, a type of hypodermic needle loaded with a premeasured dose of epinephrine that they could quickly administer to Derek Jr. if he mistakenly ingested nuts.

The incident also forced Athelia and Derek to reevaluate the hectic pace of their life. They realized that in their eagerness to care for their children while each earning a full-time paycheck, they were putting an enormous strain on the two people most needed to maintain this creaking structure—themselves. They had to create some time for each other, otherwise there wouldn't be a family at all.

On one of Derek's days off, Monday or Thursday, they arranged for a grandparent or sitter to come in for a few hours after Athelia arrived home from work. The two of them could then go out for an early supper and have time to review the week and catch up with each other. On Sundays after church, instead of going home to do more chores before Derek reported to work, they planned short outings at a local playground or, in warm weather, at the lake, where they could enjoy the children's antics in a relaxed way. Just these few hours each week gave them a break from the relentless schedule. They began to feel proud of how well they had handled the responsibilities in their lives, and also to realize that the younger children would be in school in a few years and that the pressure would ease.

"Tag-team" parenting, which some call "split-shift" parenting, is an effective way of eliminating parents' child-care dilemma. If both parents work full-time but during different shifts, they can often raise their children with little or no child care.

If parents aren't careful, however, this hectic pace can put a big strain on a marriage. Going days without seeing each other, or seeing one's spouse only while one is racing in the door from work while the spouse is racing out the door leaves little time or opportunity for face-to-face communication or intimacy.

It's very hard to provide what children need when parents themselves are becoming tense. When you're always racing the clock and feeling continually anxious, nervous, or annoyed, it interferes with the relaxation and calm you need in order to engage in dialogue or play imaginatively with your child.

Just as children need floor time with their parents, parents need "floor time" with each other. They need to spend time regularly nurturing each other, listening to each other's cares and concerns, talking about things that interest each other—just as they would focus on what interests their child during floor time with that child. It's hard to give to others what you aren't getting yourself. Husbands and wives need closeness and understanding in order to nurture their children. When you're working out complex arrangements around work and family, you need to remember that you have needs, too, and that your needs are an important part of the family as well. For tag-team parents, finding that time to be together is even more essential. A tag-team parenting arrangement goes much more smoothly when parents have at least an hour or two of overlap time each day and an evening a week by themselves. Indeed, this is a bare minimum needed to maintain a relationship under the challenging circumstances. The same nurturing, communication, and empathy that are so important for children are the cornerstones of healthy relationship between parents.

This may sound as though I've just added to parents' burden by urging that they find time not only for their children but also for each other. Actually, I believe it will make their job as parents and partners easier. Parents need time to think about their goals—why they got married and had children. Taking time for each other is a way to help set priorities—love, work, caring—and provide balance in life. Parents needn't wait for children to grow up to begin asking "What is most important to me, to us?"

This is helpful advice for parents, even if they're not "tag-team parenting." A family that has too many activities—even if all the activities are healthy, educational, and self-esteem-boosting—is in danger of missing out on the warmth and emotional sustenance that comes simply from being together.

Divorced but Making It Work

Friends and family had cautioned them that they weren't very compatible, but Grace Piantadosi and Jeff Lopez ignored the warnings. Grace, a 30-year-old electrical engineer, and Jeff, a 28-year-old drummer in a small rock band, had met at a club where Jeff was performing, and the attraction was powerful. A small, brisk woman with blond hair and a perky smile, Grace found Jeff's laid-back warmth and humor a refreshing change from the intense, serious engineers she'd been dating. Jeff, with shaggy dark hair and a short beard, was impressed by Grace's energy and ambition. Their relationship took an abrupt turn, however, after they had been dating for several months: Grace discovered she was pregnant. Raised as a Catholic, Grace could not bring herself to terminate the pregnancy, and after some heavy discussions, she and Jeff decided to make a go of it. They were married in a short ceremony in Grace's condo.

After their daughter, Rebecca, was born, tensions between the couple began to rise. Grace had expected to cut back to part-time after her maternity leave, but discovered that Jeff's income was erratic and not as high as she expected. Underlying incompatibilities between the couple began to emerge. Jeff began to find Grace's crisp, efficient manner annoying, while Grace was irritated by Jeff's nonchalant attitude toward life.

"We are as different as God could make any two people," she told friends. "We fight about everything, even the most idiotic things."

The only thing they seemed to have in common was their mutual adoration of little Rebecca. Jeff, who had a son from a previous relationship, was enchanted by his daughter. She had his big brown eyes and was, at first, totally bald. Jeff took her for strolls in her carriage on the walkways around Grace's condo, where he'd have a cigarette and show off his "little cue ball" to the old ladies out for their daily walks.

Grace, on the other hand, fretted when Jeff disappeared with the baby. She didn't want him to smoke around Rebecca, and although he insisted he didn't do so, Grace knew that when they returned Rebecca would smell of cigarette smoke.

The friction continued as Grace's four-month maternity leave drew to an end. She'd wanted to return to work part-time, and to continue breast-feeding Rebecca, but Jeff's sporadic paychecks were not enough to make ends meet. He played in some clubs in New York City, but that didn't pay well. He'd had some modest success as a studio musician for commercials, but didn't much like the work and only did it when a buddy needed his help. The couple had some bitter arguments: Grace complained of Jeff's "passive" attitude toward life, and Jeff accused Grace of a "hard-assed" outlook.

Grace was angry and despondent over her contentious marriage. Her parents had had a deeply troubled relationship and had divorced when she was a teenager. This had affected Grace deeply. She assumed that by working industriously and keeping her life in order, she would be able to avoid her parents' mistakes. She came from a large family—two brothers and three sisters—

and her mother stayed home with the children while her father earned a sporadic living as an attorney. Grace and the other children adored him, but he drank heavily and, it became clear, had numerous affairs. Grace's mother put up with her husband's behavior for years, scolding him continually for his drinking and womanizing and telling the children that she stayed in the marriage for their sake. Finally, when Grace, the oldest, was 16, her mother filed for divorce. Grace prided herself on having avoided the mistakes her mother had made, but she was beginning to think that in marrying Jeff she'd made the same mistake as her mother.

Jeff had had a more stable upbringing but, ironically, had not settled down much as an adult. His parents ran a small restaurant in New York City, where Jeff learned to love music and play the drums. He graduated from City College in New York and afterwards traveled around the country playing in this band or that. He did some work as a backup musician in Los Angeles and then moved back to the New York City area to start up his rock band. It had some modest success, but the income Jeff earned from it certainly wasn't enough to support a family. Jeff was deeply resentful at the patronizing way Grace's family and friends treated him, and he was beginning to suspect that his wife felt the same way.

With her logical engineer's mind, Grace faced facts: Her maternity leave was ending. Even though she dreaded being separated from Rebecca so soon and being plunged back into full-time work, she knew she couldn't afford to stay home full-time.

Jeff, for his part, was determined that Grace wouldn't push him aside as a father. This had happened to him in his earlier marriage. He already sensed that he was being shouldered out. Whenever he changed Rebecca's diapers, Grace hurried into the room to correct him and to rewrap the diaper more tightly. She chastised him when he gave Rebecca a supplementary bottle.

"She's getting too much air," Grace would scold, tilting the bottle up to a more upright angle. When he came home late at night after a gig, he often found Rebecca and Grace sound asleep in the bedroom. Rebecca would be wound tightly in Grace's arms, forcing Jeff to retreat to the couch.

The couple weathered their first major crisis when Grace was able to persuade her boss to allow her to work at home. She knew she was fortunate; the company she worked for was growing fast, and she was a valued employee. Grace found her boss to be surprisingly open to her proposal that she "telecommute" to her office, 35 miles away. The company supplied her with a computer, and Grace made arrangements to spend one day a week in the company's office. With that, she went back to work, and the couple settled into an uneasy routine. Grace woke up with Rebecca and fed her breakfast. They played and went for a walk until Jeff awoke midmorning and took over. Grace retreated to a small room they had fixed up as an office, although she checked in frequently with Jeff and Rebecca.

As for Rebecca, she was an alert, energetic baby who seemed to throw herself at the world. She learned to grab for things—toys, Daddy's nose, Mommy's hair, bowls of hot soup—early on, and Grace and Jeff soon learned to move anything remotely harmful as far out of reach as possible. As soon as she was able, Rebecca was on the go—scrambling, crawling, and trying to stand by reaching for anything in sight to steady herself on. She had enormous energy, needing relatively little sleep and taking only cat-naps during the day.

Keeping track of her was exhausting, Grace and Jeff found, and they were so absorbed in keeping Rebecca out of trouble that their problems with each other were put on the back burner.

"The more tired she gets, the faster she moves," Grace remarked to her mother. "She just seems to try to outrun fatigue."

They found that Rebecca loved physical games—being swung up into the air by Daddy or twirled around by Mommy. She would throw back her head and crow with delight as the world whirled by. She loved whizzing down the slide at the playground, the faster the better. Swing rides weren't any good unless she was going high and fast.

"The kid's going to be an astronaut," Jeff boasted to friends at Rebecca's first birthday party as the birthday girl merrily charged into the stomachs of the other party guests—adults and children. "She's already shooting for the moon."

In some ways, Rebecca's assertive, action-oriented personality was easier for Jeff to deal with, and harder on Grace. When Rebecca got into trouble, Grace's first instinct was to crouch down next to her daughter and earnestly try to explain why Rebecca shouldn't grab the tablecloth or throw spoons or sit on the floor and bang the back of her head into the kitchen door. In keeping with her engineering background, Grace wanted order and structure, so she found Rebecca a challenge to everything she stood for.

"Sweetheart," Grace would say nicely with a big smile. "It's very *loud* when you bang your head against the door. See? Bang!" she gently swatted her hand against the door. "So why don't you let Mommy give you a ball to play with. See? We can roll it back and forth like this and play a game. Here, you roll it to me—"

But Rebecca was too busy imitating Grace's slap at the door by delightedly pounding the door with her fist, making even more noise. "Me bang!" she said. "Me bang!"

Jeff, on the other hand, wasted little time explaining things. To him, she was like an enthusiastic drummer who loved to play interesting rhythms, and he could easily see the organization in that. At the same time, he wasn't hesitant about pulling rank when he needed to.

"Rebecca," he would say sternly when she lay on her back and kicked her legs against the wall. His voice tone dropped, and he dropped his eyebrows over his eyes. "Stop that."

If Rebecca ignored him, he would drop in front of her and eye her toughly. "Are you listening to me?" he would say again, although a note of levity would make it clear that what she was doing wasn't *that* earth-shattering. Often, Rebecca would sigh and stand up and head off in another direction.

Grace was frustrated by Rebecca's apparent disregard of her efforts to discipline her. "She doesn't seem to want to listen to me," she thought, feeling resentful that Rebecca seemed to behave better for Jeff than for her. Gradually, the tension over Rebecca's behavior served to sever the last remaining ties between Grace and Jeff and, by the time Rebecca was two years old, they had decided to divorce. Jeff moved back in with his parents across the river in New York City until he figured out what to do next.

The fight over custody of Rebecca proved deeper and uglier than either Jeff or Grace had expected. Grace assumed that since she was Rebecca's mother and since she had a more stable job and predictable income, she would almost automatically be granted custody of her daughter. Indeed, she had begun interviewing for a nanny to care for Rebecca while she worked when her attorney brought her up short, giving her a no-nonsense lesson in the realities of today's divorce courts.

"Judges these days don't just give mothers full custody and make Dad put up with every-other-weekend visitation," he warned Grace. "Unless Jeff makes it clear that he will not be an involved father, you two are going to end up with joint physical custody, which means splitting Rebecca's time between you fifty–fifty."

Grace was horrified. "But he's living with his parents above a restaurant! What does the judge expect him to do with her when he goes out at night? Sometimes he doesn't get home until four o'clock in the morning!"

Her lawyer shrugged. "As long as Jeff can find suitable child care, and this would include his parents, a judge isn't going to exclude him simply because of an unusual work schedule. Lots of parents these days have unusual work arrangements, and they manage to juggle kids."

Indeed, Jeff was determined not to be left out of Rebecca's life. He sensed that Grace would try to elbow him aside, and he vowed not to let that happen. His mother agreed to watch Grace in the morning while Jeff slept, and then he planned to take over Rebecca's care until he put her to bed before heading off to the clubs for work.

The resulting clash turned into an expensive court battle. The harder Grace argued that Jeff's lifestyle wasn't suitable for a child, the deeper Jeff dug in his heels. He also aimed for full custody, arguing that his mother was a more suitable caretaker than any nanny that Grace would hire.

In the end, a judge had to impose a settlement. His verdict: joint custody. Rebecca, he decreed, would live with her mother three and a half days a week, including weekends because of her father's heavy weekend work schedule, and then would live with her father three and a half days a week. He split the holidays down the middle.

Grace was grief-stricken at the judge's order. For several days, she stayed home from work and just wept. She simply couldn't understand why the judge had given Jeff half—*half*—of Rebecca's time when it was clear that he wasn't in a position to support her that much. What would he do with her while he was at work? His mother was busy in the restaurant in the evenings; she couldn't watch Rebecca all the time. Grace briefly considered appealing the judge's order, but eventually decided to end the battle, although she decided to remain alert and head back into court the instant she sensed that Jeff's care of Rebecca was lagging.

In this way, Rebecca began her life as a child in two households. Despite their differences, Jeff and Grace were both devoted to Rebecca. Jeff was a little amused by Grace's intensity about her daughter. He knew this intensity was part of his ex-wife's personality, but he also sensed there was an element of competitiveness in it as well. Grace didn't want to be shown up as a parent, Jeff noted. And, he realized, neither did he.

Rebecca's routine settled into weekends, Mondays, and part of Tuesdays at her mom's house and then Tuesday afternoons, Wednesdays, Thursdays, and Fridays at her dad's. Grace picked Rebecca up Friday night before Jeff took off for his gig, and Jeff dropped by Grace's house on Tuesday afternoons to pick her back up.

Grace arranged her work to fit the visitation schedule: She took Mondays and Tuesday mornings off to be with Rebecca and then worked extra long days the rest of the week to make up for it. Grace was eternally grateful to have a flexible employer who would allow such an arrangement. She and Rebecca played lots of pretend games. Rebecca continued to be an active child, and it was a challenge to keep her focused on any one activity. Grace found that she really had to be very animated or Rebecca simply lost interest and trotted off to another diversion.

"Rebecca, sweetheart, come back, we're still playing dolls," Grace would call after Rebecca raced off when she heard a car start outside. Grace found that Rebecca preferred more active games, like pretending to be a fish at the playground and running around the equipment making believe she was wiggling among rocks under water.

Grace realized that, in order to be closer to her daughter, she had to join her creative energies in an active way. During these animated pretend play sessions, not only did the two grow closer but also Grace was helping Rebecca focus and concentrate, learn to use words and ideas, and even talk about feelings. "You spilled my tea, Momma," Rebecca would shriek when she got a little older.

"Hmmm, I wonder how you feel about that," Grace would comment casually.

"I mad!" was the answer.

As for Jeff, he found he missed Rebecca and was always ready to pick her up by Tuesday afternoon, although by Friday night he was ready for a break. He was still living with his parents, who took turns watching her at night if Jeff needed to go out to a club.

Sometimes Rebecca and Jeff played games involving dancing and running, but Jeff also found himself taking on much of the role of a more soothing, comforting parent. Often Rebecca and Jeff hung out in quieter ways, watching videotapes together or looking at picture books. They listened to music together. Jeff was pleased that he was able to communicate to Rebecca a love and respect for music when she was still so young.

As close as she was to both parents, Rebecca still showed some signs of tension as she moved back and forth between the two households. She became more easily agitated and began to have some trouble falling asleep at night. Sometimes, when she got older and was able to communicate better, she said she had "scary pictures" in her head when she slept. Often, they were about losing something, such as a favorite toy, and sometimes a "mean monster" was taking away something of hers.

Over time, as Rebecca moved into the preschool years and could verbalize her feelings a bit more, she began expressing her desire to see the other parent after a day or two of separation. While at Jeff's house, she would ask if they could "visit Mommy." At Grace's, she demanded that she "make Daddy come here now." This was hard on Grace and Jeff. Their divorce had been so bitter that they avoided seeing each other as much as possible. Finally, begrudgingly, they gave in—a bit. They both began stopping by for a quick hello to Rebecca at the church where she had started attending morning nursery school in New York City. Jeff dropped by on the days when Rebecca was otherwise with Grace, and Grace came on Jeff's days. It wasn't a perfect solution, but it was the best they could live with under the circumstances. Rebecca got what she needed—a daily dose of Momma and Papa—and Grace and Jeff got what they wanted—an opportunity for a daily dose of their daughter without the daily trauma of seeing each other.

Jeff and Grace's story illustrates that a version of the Four-Thirds Solution can work even for divorced parents. Although it certainly isn't easy, it is possible for divorced parents like Grace and Jeff, whose relationship with each other isn't very good, to give their child the nurturing and attention that she needs. Despite their differences, Grace and Jeff were able to work out a solution using flexible work schedules and family members.

If Grace and Jeff could have worked out a long-term relationship, Rebecca might have benefited from the yin-yang balance of both parents—Daddy providing encouragement for her unbridled energy and Mommy providing the necessary balance with organization and structure.

Unless both parents have been involved from the beginning, until the age of two or three, it can be difficult for a child to be away from a primary parent, even for just half the week. In these situations, I usually recommend that the child not spend more than one night away from the primary, or custodial, parent. In Grace and Jeff's case, they had joint physical custody. I would have preferred it if the judge had declared one or the other to be the custodial parent.

Before noncustodial parents react in horror at this comment, let me add quickly that this doesn't mean that the noncustodial parent needs to stay away! Not by a long shot. Children need *frequent* contact with each parent *daily*. Noncustodial parents can have the children for as many full days as have been agreed upon, but it's best for children if they return almost every night to the home of the parent with physical custody. Ideally, a baby or toddler shouldn't spend more than one night a week away from the custodial parent. The noncustodial parent should try for rights to visit every day.

Obviously, this means that divorced parents need to live fairly close together; obviously, this strategy won't work if parents live in different cities or states. In those cases, daily phone calls and frequent visits are important. But I'll be frank. It's best for children to have daily contact with each parent. If you are divorced and have young children, you may want to consider staying near or moving closer to your children, if that's at all possible. At the very least, think long and hard if you've been offered a promotion or new job that would take you many miles away from your children. I know that this is not always easy for parents, but the truth is that children need both their parents, especially during those crucial early years.

When a divorce has been particularly rancorous and bitter or where there has been abuse, it may be too much to expect that each parent will allow the other parent to visit on a daily basis. Of course, I would hope that parents could work out their differences for the sake of the children, but when they can't be worked out, then other ways should be sought for a child to see each parent every day. For example, the custodial parent that day could step out of the home when the other parent arrives, or remain in a separate room. If a grandparent, nanny, or day-care center is caring for the child, the parent can visit then. I would not urge the parents into daily encounters with an ex-spouse when those encounters are extremely uncomfortable. Rather, my point is to encourage parents to work out an arrangement where the child can see each parent every day—and to be as creative as they can to accomplish that goal.

If parents live near each other, later on, when children are old enough, it's good if they can bike or walk between Mommy's house and Daddy's house. Or they might take the school bus to Dad's and have Mom pick them up after dinner. Often parents informally work out these arrangements for practical reasons. One parent may transport the children to after-school team practices and music lessons while the other parent picks them up from those activities. Splitting activities in this way can give both parents almost daily access to their children even when the children are splitting their weeks between parents.

If both parents are very close to their children, and if their children are equally secure with both parents, then it's much easier for children to spend a few days with one parent and a few days with the other parent. But it's still hard on them because children would prefer it if both the people they love and depend on were available each day. Indeed, it's rare that a child feels an equal amount of security with both parents at this early age. Giving them that security means some sacrifices from parents. But it is hard to think of a more worthwhile goal.

A Traditional Family Adapts

It was the last straw—utterly and completely. Stacey Kim took a look around her kitchen—the upturned milk carton dripping its contents off the table, the bowl of cereal lying upside down on the floor, the sink full of dishes, the streaked cabinets, the scribbled-on walls, the overflowing garbage can, and the three wide-eyed children staring at her in stunned silence—and sat down, put her head on the crowded table and sobbed.

She thought in despair: Stacey Kim, former interior designer and currently desperate mother of three and wife of workaholic lawyer Spencer Kim—what a picture. If only her affluent, successful clients could see her now. Messy house, messy kids, messy life. A life that revolved around diapers, bottles, nursery school, playgrounds, Teletubbies. After six years, it was getting to be much too much. She'd expected to be so happy when she met Spencer eight years ago! Both the children of Korean immigrants, they grew up in the Los Angeles suburbs and met while Stacey was enjoying her budding career in interior design and Spencer was launching his career in corporate law. Now here they were, three children later—Meghan was six, Kaitlin was three, and James was one—and Stacey was going out of her mind.

It had all happened so fast this morning. Meghan and Kaitlin got into a fight over who knows what. They were fighting a lot these days. At any rate, one of the two of them threw a spoon, and it hit James in his high chair in his eye. He threw himself back in his chair, knocking his bowl of cereal onto the floor at the same time that Meghan knocked over the milk, which spilled onto Kaitlin. By the time it was all over, the kitchen was a wreck, and Kaitlin, James, and, finally, Stacey had burst into tears. Stacey's outburst surprised the children so much that Kaitlin and James stopped crying to watch their sobbing mother, with her face on the kitchen table.

"Mommy?" Meghan, the oldest, asked cautiously. This was a new situation. Mommy was usually so calm and soothing.

At the kitchen table, Stacey fought to calm herself. It had been a hard couple of weeks. Spencer was working on a tough case and had been working 18-hour days. Not that it was much different at other times. Spencer worked for a high-profile law firm and hadn't yet made partner, so long hours were fairly routine for him.

This wasn't what she had bargained for, Stacey thought, as she finally stopped crying and blew her nose with a used paper napkin she found on the cluttered kitchen table. She settled the kids in front of a video and tackled the dirty kitchen. She had grown up assuming she would marry, have several children, and stay home to raise them. Some of her friends had talked about careers in the law, academia, and the corporate world, but Stacey knew she would take a long break in her career for her kids. While in high school, she realized she had a real gift for style and color and settled on interior design as a career. It was also a career that she could leave and return to, she knew, when she had finished raising her family.

Stacey's plan had worked well—until recently. She had met Spencer through friends, and they had liked each other instantly. Even though they were both thoroughly Americanized, they liked the fact that each had also been raised in the Korean culture. Both spoke fluent Korean, and Stacey was an excellent Korean cook. As Spencer and Stacey got to know each other, they realized they shared the same values. They both wanted several children—three or four—and they wanted to raise them so they understood and appreciated their Korean background. Like Stacey, Spencer felt it was important that the children have a parent at home, and Stacey was relieved. Other men she'd dated had assumed that their wives would work outside the home so they could maintain the same standard of living after they had children. If fact, she had ended a couple of relationships after realizing that the men would not accept a stay-at-home wife.

Stacey and Spencer were married in a traditional Korean ceremony in Los Angeles with 150 friends and family in attendance, and Stacey quickly found herself pregnant. They bought a small bungalow in a Los Angeles suburb that Stacey decorated inexpensively but beautifully in soft shades of grays, blues, and mauves and with furniture that she bought at yard sales and antique stores and then refinished and refurbished.

The first few years of pregnancies and babies were blissful—the way Stacey had always dreamed it would be. Her routine revolved around her children and her home. She made friends with the other at-home moms in the neighborhood. She joined the local La Leche League group for breast-feeding mothers and also a couple of weekday-morning groups for mothers of young children. With Meghan and Kaitlin, she went to Gymboree and the local library and spent leisurely mornings in the park. She barely noticed the long hours that Spencer was putting in. He wouldn't have a chance to make partner for several years; in the meantime, as he told his wife, he would have to "bust my behind," to make sure he made partner. The hours wouldn't get much better after he made partner, of course, but at least the salary would rise exponentially.

But by the time James came along, Stacey noticed that Spencer seemed to be finding more and more reasons not to come home. He seemed to be thrown by the increasing chaos on the home front. He had been an only child, and Stacey wondered whether all this was too much for him.

Stacey found herself shouldering more and more of the burden. Whereas before, when Spencer got home before the kids went to bed, he would give one or two of the children a bath, now he busied himself with a household chore that, he told Stacey, had to be done. Or he offered to clean up the kitchen, insisting that Stacey needed a break from cleaning, while Stacey bathed the kids or put them to bed. On weekends, he started playing golf— a sport he had always said he hated. But now he had to play with clients, he told Stacey. It was part of the job. He bought a set of golf clubs and started practicing his swing in the backyard before he went to work while Stacey got the kids up. If he wanted to make partner, these were the kinds of things he had to do, he said.

Stacey was skeptical, but she didn't want to confront Spencer. She struggled with her resentment. What did she know about the corporate world, she kept trying to tell herself. This must be the way things work in that world.

But by the time James was walking, Stacey was beginning to lose it. Gone were the leisurely mornings at the playground. Now at the playground she had to chase James and Kaitlin—both daredevils—around to make sure they didn't fall off the top of the slide on their heads. At home, the children squabbled constantly. Kaitlin hated naps, so Stacey lost her middle-of-the-day break. After James stopped nursing, Stacey stopped going to her La Leche League meetings. And her mothers-group meetings weren't as fun because she was constantly roaming the room supervising her two youngest rather than sitting cross-legged on the floor enjoying conversations with the other mothers.

At home, things were a mess. Stacey, who had always prided herself on maintaining a tidy home environment, just couldn't keep up with three clutter-producing children. The house began to deteriorate, and she felt as though she were drowning.

Stacey loved being very close to her children, but she missed adult companionship. Spencer was away so much, and even when he was home, he might as well be at the office. If he wasn't practicing his golf swing, he was up in the bedroom on his laptop reading his e-mail and working on legal briefs. Stacey missed her friends from work. She missed being creative. She missed going out after work and having a margarita with coworkers. She missed having a life. Stacey and Spencer's sex life—always robust—began to decline as Spencer withdrew into his work

One evening after the children were asleep, Stacey let Spencer know that she felt isolated and overwhelmed. The intensity with which she poured out these feelings took him by surprise. Since there were no easy solutions, they decided to get a sitter for one evening each weekend, to have time to talk things over. Meanwhile

Stacey made arrangements to meet and have lunch with a few friends who were also at-home moms, to get a little perspective. She was surprised but relieved to hear that many of her friends felt the same way. Husbands tended to become absorbed in their work, leaving wives feeling isolated and lonely.

After some discussion, Spencer agreed to cut back on his golf and spend more time with the children. He began taking the kids to the playground every Saturday morning, where he got to know the other dads who were also giving their wives a break. To his surprise, it wasn't as chaotic and out of control as he had expected it to be. In fact, he kind of liked playing around with the kids at the park. He found a McDonald's nearby with an indoor playground, where he could have a cup of coffee and an Egg McMuffin while the kids played in the mesh enclosure filled with hundreds of plastic balls. Meghan kept an eye on her younger brother and sister while they whooped and dove in and out of the plastic balls.

After taking some interior design classes on Saturday mornings as a refresher, Stacey made plans for part-time work. She began to feel like a member of the adult world again, she told Spencer. She lined up a baby-sitter two mornings a week and began to work with a couple of clients again, advising them on projects such as home remodelings and kitchen redesigns.

An architect friend with a large nearby office agreed to rent office space to Stacey and to refer small design jobs to her. Slowly, Stacey began to feel less desperate and frantic about everything. She began to realize that it was okay to keep her hand in her career—in fact, when she looked around at her at-home friends, she noticed that they, too, hadn't dropped out completely. Two former lawyers taking time out of their careers to be at home with their children kept in touch with colleagues, retained memberships in professional organizations, and took on occasional short-term legal projects, for example. A speech therapist friend who was home with her two children had kept two private clients—just enough to keep her hand in her profession, and a writer did an occasional article for a local magazine. True, Stacey had other friends who had dropped completely out of the profession—in fact, she didn't even know what they had done in the working world before they had become mothers. But Stacey felt more kinship with the friends who kept a link to their professional lives. Her part-time work kept her confident that someday, when she was ready, more work would be there waiting for her. But for now, there were the children.

Stacey's story is a familiar one, even more familiar to an earlier generation of mothers who assumed that they would stay home when their children were young, but found the same sense of isolation closing in. Stacey made a more conscious decision to stay home than those earlier mothers, but still found that her plans, and Spencer's, needed adjusting.

When the raising of children is not looked upon as a joint venture, resentment can begin to brew, as it did in the Kim household. This imbalance can color both the relationship between the parents and their relationship with the children, unless the issues are addressed openly as Stacey did. Sometimes the stay-at-home parent turns to so-called gate-keeping, keeping the other parent out of the children's lives entirely in a territorial manner. Sometimes the parent who is out at work gets to interact with the children only as a disciplinarian or provider of treats. In all such situations, the children usually miss out on the sense that their parents are a team, committed to them as the top priority.

Fortunately the Kims, especially Stacey, saw the situation developing and they worked on it together. By cooperating they serve their children well as role models; in addition, the traditional values they seek to preserve will also offer their children an anchor in a changing world.

Working at Home

When friends remark enviously on Eileen Ochs's child-care arrangement or compliment her on having such a flexible husband, Eileen smiles inwardly. Little do they know the long, hard struggle she and her husband have waged to get to this point. After the experiences they endured putting their older child in day care, their current arrangement is the only way they could figure out how to have another child and still keep their sanity.

Eileen and John have two children, six-year-old Victoria and one-year-old Gabriel. Victoria is in first grade and attends an afternoon program at her school until five-thirty, when Eileen, who works at a pediatrician's office nearby, picks her up. Gabriel stays home during the day and is cared for by John, who doubles as child-care provider and co-breadwinner in the dual-income household. A photographer who works out of the family home, John, 29, cares for Gabriel while running his photography business. Whether developing film in his darkroom, picking up supplies, or calling on clients, John is usually accompanied by Gabriel.

The couple's unusual arrangement didn't usually arise out of any desire to plow new ground in the national debate over how working parents can accommodate children. But John and Eileen's willingness to experiment, and their struggles to make their arrangement work, could well inspire others to come up with creative ways of integrating work and children. Raising children in a comfortable and healthy way doesn't mean making black-and-white choices or choices that are fixed for many years. Parents don't need to choose between staying home with their children all the time and working long hours away from their children.

Eileen and John's story starts out conventionally enough. Eileen, an administrative assistant, and John, a medical photographer, grew up in the Washington area. They came from modest family backgrounds. Eileen's father was a postal worker and her mother was a church secretary for a small Catholic parish. John's dad worked for the state government, and his mother stayed home with John and his two brothers. Neither family had money for college tuition. After high school, Eileen took an administrative assistant's course and started out with a job as a receptionist at a doctor's office in downtown Washington. John worked his way through a local community college, took courses in medical photography, and was able to land a job at a medical school in the Washington area.

Like many couples, John and Eileen struggled financially. In the high-priced suburbs, their salaries didn't go far. They bought a modest townhouse in a slightly run-down suburb about 40 miles south of Washington. An added financial burden was Eileen's ailing mother. Eileen's dad had died several years previously, and her mother had retired from her job because of ill health and was trying to live on a small pension. It wasn't easy, and Eileen and her four brothers and sisters often pitched in to cover some of their mother's medical bills and living expenses.

When Victoria came along, things got even tighter for John and Eileen. Eileen's office didn't offer paid maternity leave, so Eileen went back to work after she'd used the four weeks of sick leave she'd accumulated. John took two weeks of vacation after Eileen went back to work to be with Victoria, but then he, too, had to return to his job. So John and Eileen had made arrangements for Victoria to be cared for in the day by a local baby-sitter.

Victoria didn't adjust well to child care. She cried frequently when she was dropped off at her baby-sitter's, and after she was picked up at the end of the day she alternated between being very withdrawn and crying. When her first baby-sitter moved out of the area, John and Eileen found a family child-care provider, but this arrangement lasted only a few months, because this woman found a job outside the home. The couple then turned to Eileen's mother, but after only a few weeks she told them that Victoria was too much for her. In the hopes of finding more continuity of care, John and Eileen then enrolled Victoria in a nearby child-care center.

The constant changes were hard on Victoria. Every time her day care changed, Victoria was upset for months. She cried hysterically when she was dropped off and had to be pried off her mother before Eileen could leave for work. It was a wrenching experience, and Eileen finally had to ask John to take over the drop-off because she was arriving at work too emotionally wrung out to concentrate. In the evening, Victoria seemed withdrawn and uninterested in playing. By the time Friday came, Victoria seemed to grow more accustomed to her routine, and she wouldn't cry so much. But then after a weekend with her parents, she would again become extremely upset when returning to child care on Monday.

Eileen and John tried to tell themselves that once they got Victoria settled in a day-care arrangement and stopped moving her around as much, Victoria would settle down. And Victoria, now two, did seem a bit more comfortable at the day-care center, although John and Eileen weren't very happy with it. The employees in the baby rooms and toddler rooms, which were separated from each other by only a short wall, seemed overwhelmed by the cacophony created by eight babies and 12 toddlers in the small space. The cries of the babies and the shrieks of the toddlers seemed to bounce off the wall and amplify in volume. Eileen noticed that the caregivers rarely sat down to play with the children. Instead, they gazed off into space or talked amongst each other until a baby cried or the toddlers began squabbling over a toy. Then they simply picked up the baby and offered her a bottle, or moved the toddlers apart from one another.

Victoria began to show some worrisome behavior. Eileen noticed that when she was frustrated—when another child took a toy she wanted—or sad when Eileen left for work—she would turn those feelings into aggression. Instead of finding another toy or activity, she pushed and scratched. Child-care workers complained occasionally about her biting and hitting other children when she was frustrated, and Eileen and John noticed the behavior at home. When Eileen and John were talking, and Victoria wanted a hug or cuddle, she dissolved into a temper tantrum if either of her parents didn't respond instantly.

At first, Eileen and John dismissed their daughter's development as perfectly normal. Every time a worker in their daughter's day-care center quit and another joined, they looked hopefully for a better atmosphere. For a while, the situation improved when Jan, a new lead teacher, came to Victoria's toddler class. She was a former elementary school teacher who was reentering the workforce now that her children were in high school. A short woman with warm brown eyes and a generous smile, Jan soon won over all the toddlers. She sat on the floor and played with them, gazing into their faces and dispensing lots of hugs and kisses. Soon she had the rambunctious toddlers singing simple songs and playing games like "Duck, Duck, Goose" and "Who Stole the Cookie from the Cookie Jar." Jan also encouraged the children in her group to engage in pretend play; she brought in some old clothes from her home for the children to dress up in. They held pretend "tea parties" with their stuffed animals, and played games outside in which Jan pretended to be the big, bad wolf chasing the little sheep. The children were delighted when they each got to take a turn being the big, bad wolf. Victoria started to look forward to going to "my school," and Eileen and John began to hope that their daughter had turned the corner.

Victoria's vocabulary grew by leaps and bounds, and she seemed less frustrated and aggressive at day care as well as at home. Her pretend play began to expand. She pretended she was Cinderella and clomped around the house in a pair of Eileen's pumps and a slip, tapping people on the head with her "wand" (an old spatula) when they bent down to her. She was less apt to hit John or Eileen when she was frustrated, and her temper tantrums began to subside as she was more able to articulate her feelings.

She still wept when John or Eileen left her at day care, but now she would cling to their legs only briefly, saying, "Don't leave!" and then seemed to cheer up when John or Eileen told her they would be back to pick her up after work. She waved at the door, saying, "I see you after you go work" before turning to absorb herself in play with "Miss Jan."

But after only six months, Jan moved on. She got a job as a kindergarten teacher in the local school system, which was facing a shortage of teachers and was hiring many child-care teachers with education degrees for double or triple their child-care salaries. John and Eileen were devastated by her departure, as was Victoria. Victoria's moods grew stormier again, and her tantrums were long and loud at home and at school. The new teacher, who seem less interested in playing games with the children and more interested in making sure they followed the rules, complained to Eileen that Victoria wouldn't participate in activities and was uncooperative.

"We need to do something," Eileen told John one day after another note from the teacher complaining about Victoria came home in her backpack.

"What?" said John. "I'm open to any ideas."

Eileen sighed. "I'm not sure, but this day-care thing just isn't working for her."

At first, John and Eileen were tempted just to ride out the latest storm—wait until the new teacher moved on, as was inevitable, and hope that Victoria had a better rapport with the next teacher.

"But what if the next teacher isn't any better? What do we do then?" Eileen asked John.

It took a lot of discussion and thought, until the couple finally concluded that Victoria needed more time at home. But how to accomplish that on their meager financial resources? John hit upon a possible solution. He noticed ads for "medical transcriptionists" in the newspaper. "Work at home," they promised. "Set your own pace."

"Couldn't you do this?" he said, pointing out the ads to Eileen. She shrugged. "I guess so. I do it in my office."

"Don't you see?" asked John. "You could quit and do this transcribing stuff at night and on weekends when I'm home to watch Victoria. You wouldn't make as much money as at your job, but we wouldn't have to have the day-care bills. And Victoria wouldn't have to go to day care."

The thought of suddenly leaving her job and plunging into self-employment didn't sit well with Eileen. She'd been brought up to believe that you held on to your job no matter what. Taking risks was too dangerous—especially when there were few financial resources to fall back on.

"No way," she said, shaking her head. "I'm not going to just quit. What if it didn't work? A month without my paycheck and we'd be dead broke. Why don't you figure out some way to bring in some extra money? Can't you do some freelance photography on the side? Then maybe I could quit or work part-time."

The suggestion reminded John of an idea he'd had several months ago when he and Eileen had attended a friend's wedding. He'd watched the photographer with interest as he moved around, quietly clicking photos of the bride, groom, and wedding party. *I could do that*, John remembered thinking. *That isn't hard. And I could do it and still keep my regular job.* He also liked photographing cheerful events, in contrast to the medical subjects he dealt with in his job.

With that idea in mind, John called a few photography friends who shot wedding photos on weekends. He picked their brains, purchased another camera, and went into business. A friend put together an elegant Web site for him. "John H. Ochs: Professional Photographer," it said, showcasing samples of his work, "Corporate, Event, Studio, and Location photography."

It took awhile, but John gradually accumulated a couple of digital cameras and built up his weekend business. At first he shot mostly small weddings, where he earned a few hundred dollars for several hours' work. But, gradually, he began to attract clients who were still interested in black-and-white photography. John slowly converted the laundry room into a darkroom, so he could supply his customers with more services. The additional darkroom work meant that the family had less time together, but Eileen accepted the trade-off because of the extra money.

After seeing the success that John was having at his weekend business, Eileen started answering the ads for medical transcriptionists. She found that her experience at the doctor's office had given her plenty of experience with a wide range of medical terms, and because she was a fast typist, she could work her way through the doctors' tapes quickly. She worked Saturday nights and Sunday afternoons when John was home or rose early to fit the work in when John was working during the weekends.

After a few months, as her reputation grew and her transcription business expanded, Eileen asked whether she could cut back to part-time at the office. The two doctors who owned the clinic were less than pleased with the request, but they didn't want to lose Eileen because she was a hard worker who had a pleasant manner with patients. So each day at 12:30, Eileen left work, picked up Victoria, then three, at the day-care center, and they went out for an afternoon together.

Once again, Victoria became a calmer, happier child. She and Eileen went to the playground a lot in the afternoon or just played around in the house. At first, it was hard on Eileen to spend so much time with Victoria. She was demanding, and Eileen sometimes longed for the relative tranquillity of her job, where she only had to satisfy two doctors instead of a three-year-old! But it was glorious to be free of the constant anxiety over Victoria, Eileen thought. After Victoria went to bed, Eileen settled down to transcribing the tapes the medical transcription office went over each week. It was a tiring routine, but at least Eileen felt better about Victoria.

After a summer of this routine, Eileen felt confident enough about her freelance work to pull Victoria from the child-care center and enroll her in a morning preschool program at a local church, where the pace was slower and teachers were geared more toward learning and play. The preschool program didn't operate in the summer, but Eileen felt secure enough with her current work that she figured she could find a solution for next summer when the time came.

Life settled down to a more pleasant routine. But when Victoria turned four, they found themselves longing for another child. They wanted Victoria to have siblings, as they had had, but they were torn. Much as they wanted another child, they had no desire to return to the stress of Victoria's early years, when Eileen and John had struggled home from their jobs only to deal with an angry, crying child night after night.

Again, the couple put their heads together, and it was John who suggested a solution. He'd built up his freelance business enough so he felt confident about striking out on his own. So what if Eileen went back to full-time work, because the family would need the stability and the medical benefits of one job, while he stayed home with the baby?

Eileen looked at him, puzzled.

"We can't afford an at-home dad."

"No," said John. "You don't get it. I'd run my business *and* take care of the baby."

"At the same *time*?" asked Eileen. "Are you nuts?"

"Maybe I am," said John. "But I think it might work. All my equipment is here. I've got the computer and the darkroom downstairs. I think I can do it."

"What will you do with the baby when you go out on jobs?" asked Eileen.

"I guess the baby will just have to come with me," John said.

It was an unusual scheme, and Eileen was doubtful it would succeed, but John seemed so confident that she went along with it.

Before long, she landed a job with a pediatrician near their home. That summer, John left his regular job to be with Victoria. In the fall, she began kindergarten and an after-school program. When Gabriel was born, Eileen took a six-week maternity leave and then headed back to work—but not without regret. She had no idea how John's arrangement was going to work. Eileen had always handled a lot of the details of the care of Victoria: she'd made the doctor's appointments, met with the day-care providers, and bought clothes and supplies. Even in the first few weeks with Gabriel, she did most of the diaper changing. This wasn't going to be easy for John, she thought, and worried that he was underestimating the gargantuan task of running his business and minding an infant. Eileen also felt torn by the idea that her husband, not she, would spend most of her son's waking hours with him.

The first few weeks with Gabriel actually went fairly smoothly for John. The baby slept in a Portacrib in John's small office on the bottom floor of their home. When awake, he liked to gaze at the shifting shadows on the wall as the sun moved across the sky and watch the toys that John strung across the top of the crib.

John felt great. "This is working," he told himself exuberantly. He hadn't wanted to let on to Eileen, but he wasn't as confident as he had acted about this arrangement. Running his own business made him nervous enough. Add to that the care and feeding of a newborn, and his stress level had shot off the charts. He had nightmares of talking on the phone with his most important client and having Gabriel suddenly start screaming furiously. Grappling with a squealing baby and a client at the same time . . . John didn't even want to think about what would happen to his business. All the familiar tasks of his daily routine—doing shoots for clients in their homes or offices or in the cramped studio next to his office, processing prints in the darkroom that doubled as a laundry room, examining proofs, talking to clients on the telephone, editing his digital photos on the computer—had to be rethought with Gabriel in mind.

What would he do with the baby while he was in the darkroom? He'd had some vague idea of leaving Gabriel out in the Portacrib while he developed film, but soon realized that was impractical. Every time Gabriel squawked, he'd have to leave the darkroom to check on him—but that was impossible because it would mean opening the door and letting in light. Fortunately, with his digital cameras, more and more of John's "developing" work was actually being done with the computer and printer. Eventually, for the limited time he had to spend in the darkroom, John installed an elaborate ventilation system that protected them both from any fumes, then tucked Gabriel into his infant seat and brought him into the darkroom with him.

"Here we go, little fellow," he said the first time, as he sat Gabriel's baby carrier on top of the dryer and turned to his equipment. "It's do or die, little guy."

To John's amazement, Gabriel seemed quite comfortable. As John snapped off the overhead light, Gabriel gazed curiously around the room in the dim light that remained. As John started up the print processor, the soft splash and whoosh from the machine filled the room, and John braced for a howl from Gabriel. But, in fact, John watched as Gabriel's eyes closed softly. He was asleep!

"It must have sounded like inside mommy," John told Eileen later. "All that sloshing around, you know."

Eileen grinned. "Whatever works. Maybe you could market the print processor as some kind of baby soother. You'd make a million dollars."

But Gabriel wasn't as mellow at other times. He fussed and fumed if left too long on his back in the playpen in John's office. John grew used to matter-of-factly telling clients on the phone, "That's my son. He's home with me for a while." The client usually laughed sympathetically. John figured the client had assumed that Gabriel was either sick or that their regular day-care arrangement had fallen through. No sense trying to explain his unusual child-care arrangement to anybody who didn't have to know, John decided.

It took John awhile to figure out Gabriel. He was kind of a prickly kid, John decided after a few days. Aside from the print processor, there didn't seem to be much else that soothed Gabriel very well. Bright lights, John discovered, sent Gabriel up the wall: he squinted and squawked under the lights in John's office, and he wasn't happy with loud noises, either; Gabriel started and looked scared every time the phone rang. What's more, Gabriel hated the baby swing—all that movement upset him even more. So for the moment, that left the dimly lit darkroom and the soft gurgling of the print processor as the only things that kept Gabriel below boiling level.

"I guess we're going to be using the regular camera instead of the digital and developing *a lot* of photos for a while," was John's grim assessment to Eileen one day early on. "That baby just cries too much otherwise."

Eileen got worried. "Is this going to work? Or should we try to think of another way to take care of him?"

John grew irritated. For God's sake, it had only been a couple of weeks, and Eileen was ready to pull the plug. To tell the truth, John was a little upset with himself for not having things more under control—but this kid, he thought, is a puzzle. Victoria hadn't been a piece of cake at this stage, but at least he hadn't had to put up with her all day long.

But John wasn't ready to quit. Not by a long shot. He was convinced that he and Gabriel would come to a meeting of the minds at some point. John just hoped it would come sooner rather than later—before all his clients bailed out after hearing Gabriel wailing in the background every time they called.

"This is going to work," he told Eileen, sounding a lot more confident than he felt. "We'll make it work. Let's not panic." Yet he did worry silently to himself.

John renewed his efforts to learn what could soothe Gabriel and how he could help Gabriel soothe himself. Starting with the clues of the darkroom and the photo processor, John realized that Gabriel was a highly sensitive baby. He didn't like a lot of noise or bright lights. A bit of stimulation went a long way, John realized.

Well, John realized, if you can't beat 'em, join 'em. So he replaced the light bulbs in his office with slightly lower-wattage bulbs, turned down the volume on the phone ringer, and squirted some WD-40 on his old filing cabinet so it didn't squeak so much when he opened the drawers. He also discovered that Gabriel loved to be stroked softly, so if John was talking to a client, he sat Gabriel on his desk in his baby seat and rubbed him softly on the tummy. When John was working with a client in his studio, he learned to leave Gabriel in his playpen with a few toys in it, around the corner from his office so the bright lights wouldn't bother him. Gabriel squealed a bit, but at least he could hear John's voice, so he didn't seem to mind waiting for him to return.

Outdoor assignments weren't as difficult. Gabriel liked the soothing hum of car rides, and when he was a little older and able to hold his head up, he happily rode around in a backpack. The kid wants to see the world, John thought fondly.

As for explaining the constant presence of his son to clients, John soon learned that less was more. People weren't interested in complicated explanations from a photographer they barely knew as to why he had a pint-sized sidekick, so John didn't give many. He learned to introduce Gabriel briefly. "Here's my son, Gabriel. He's helping me out today," and let people draw their own conclusions. Regular clients soon grew accustomed to Gabriel, and new clients didn't much care after they realized that John was used to working with Gabriel on board. Weddings weren't a problem because Eileen was home on weekends. He got a baby-sitter if the shoot was going to be complicated or time-consuming. But most people didn't have a lot of time these days to stand around and smile for a photographer, John realized, so he shot fast and left quickly. After a few months, John felt much better about the new arrangement. He did occasionally worry that he might be missing out on some assignments because people couldn't deal with the idea that he came equipped with camera *and* child, but he decided to view that as the client's problem. Besides, having Gabriel around sure beat paying the rates charged by a child-care center.

A bigger challenge for John was Eileen. Outside of Victoria's day-care hours, she had shouldered most of the responsibility for

Victoria, taking care of her mornings and evenings, even when she and John were working full-time. John automatically assumed that she would do the same for Gabriel. Before leaving for work, she dressed Gabriel, fed him breakfast, and left John intricate instructions on what to feed Gabriel for lunch, when to put him down for a nap, when to take him for a walk in the stroller, and dozens of other details. She called several times a day to ask pointed questions about Gabriel and his routine.

Eileen grilled him on how much he was playing with Gabriel.

"Playing with him?" John was astounded at the question. "Hey, I'm trying to run a business. I give him a quick tickle every now and then, but I'm pretty busy."

"Can't you take a few minutes every now and then and get him interested in a rattle or a toy or something," Eileen asked. "It's not good for him to just lie around and watch you."

John sighed. "Well, he seems to be pretty happy doing that, at least some of the time. But, okay, I'll try."

It was hard at first, but John forced himself to take a few minutes every hour and get down on the floor and have a few chuckles with Gabriel whenever he was awake. He would hold a rattle between his teeth and shake it, growling like a dog. Gabriel thought that was pretty funny, and he would try to grab the rattle. John also got into the habit of showing Gabriel finished prints and asking his opinion.

"So, what do you think, big guy," he would say as he pointed to a glossy photo of some corporate exec on his computer screen or in the darkroom. Gabriel would respond with big smiles and some sympathetic gurgles.

Eileen tried to persuade John to play little games with Gabriel for 15 minutes or more out of every hour—at least, when the baby was calm and alert. John tried, but he let it lapse when he got busy. Gabriel busied himself by sucking on his toes and squealing when he wanted attention.

"Did you feed him the carrots for lunch?" she'd ask. "When did he get his afternoon bottle? Don't you think a one-hour nap is kind of short? Make sure he wears his jacket when you go out today. It's supposed to get cold later in the afternoon."

At times, she even came home at lunch to inspect Gabriel to make sure things were ship-shape—or, at least, John thought resentfully, that's what it felt like, as though she was checking up on him.

Eileen was shocked, however, when John brought it up.

"I thought you'd want the help!" she said. "I was just trying to make it easier for you. There's a lot to remember when you're taking care of a baby."

"You don't make it easier for me when I have to stop to answer a couple dozen questions about Gabriel in the middle of working." John was trying not to let his irritation show. "Gabe and I are doing fine. This isn't easy, but then nothing is. He seems pretty happy, he's growing and I'm making some money. We're doing okay."

Indeed, Gabriel's face lit up when he saw John, and he seemed to prefer cuddling with his daddy rather than his mommy. He gurgled happily when Daddy tickled his tummy and he held up his arms to be held when John came into the room.

Eileen had to admit that this preference made her jealous and a little sad. "Now I don't have to worry when Gabriel or Victoria gets sick and I have to take a day off from work to stay home with them," she told her mother. "But I guess I wish I was the one at home. It's hard knowing that John's seeing everything Gabriel does before I do. I feel likes he gets the best of Gabriel, and I get what's left at the end of the day when he's cranky."

John had his own frustrations, such as when Gabriel wanted to play but John had to get some work done. There were times when he put Gabriel in front of the television set. Gabriel was too young to comprehend much of what was on TV, and at least it occupied him for a while.

At Gabriel's first birthday party, the family felt they had much to celebrate. At the same time, they looked anxiously at the future. Gabriel had learned to walk, and now John had to watch him more carefully. He was still a fussy child who didn't like a lot of stimulation, and he was just starting to throw temper tantrums when things didn't go his way. It was getting harder for John to keep an eye on him when he had clients in the studio, and Gabriel was growing highly discontented with his playpen.

"We may have to rethink this whole deal," John told Eileen one day after Gabriel's birthday party. "I can't spend a lot of time playing with him, and I don't want him to become a TV head. So let's just see how it goes and stay flexible. We may need to change things all over again."

Victoria came home on the bus each day, and John and Gabriel met her at the bus stop. She was quite helpful. John would put her in charge of entertaining the baby for an hour or so, and Victoria was pleased to have such an important job.

Eileen agreed that they might have to change their lives around again to accommodate their jobs and their growing children.

"We've done it before," she told John. "We can do it again."

This particular family's story highlights a number of issues that confront American families. Most important, it highlights what happens to some young children when care is not adequate, such as when a child-care center's staff changes constantly. In Victoria we saw a child who formed relationships with her child-care providers, only to be upset when she lost them again. She experienced more upset than any one of us would wish for our children. Instead of learning how to experience the full range of emotions, which a child is gearing up to learn, and learning to cope flexibly with these expectable feelings, she began to show what might generally be called problem behavior (what developmental psychologists call "constrictions"). At about age two, she began having tantrums. When frustrated or sad, she behaved aggressively, biting and pushing. Equally important was the fact that she wasn't developing the coping capacities we generally see in children her age. We like to see children of two and three learning to deal with their sad, frustrated, or angry feelings by either figuring out ways to get what they want or, as they get a little older, by playing out or verbalizing their feelings.

For example, a two- or three-year-old, with appropriate emotional support, can learn to get a little more demanding when she's angry instead of acting out her anger. She might show her anger but not bite or hit. Demanding behavior is behavior that is likely to change the situation making the child angry in the first place, such as another child getting more attention or feeling neglected. An example of demanding behavior would be a young preschooler who, when feeling a little sad or lonely, might learn how to behave coyly in order to draw the attention of some of the adults nearby and get some of the warmth and nurturing she wants. By the age of three or four, when they have better language skills and pretend-play skills, preschoolers who have received lots of emotional support might play out their dilemma with dolls or say directly, "I'm mad!" or "I miss Mommy!"

When a child doesn't feel secure enough to develop these healthy coping skills, she may instead express these feelings of sadness, frustration, or anger as problem behavior. Unfortunately, her biting, tantrums, or pushing then tend to dig the hole a little deeper because it usually means the child gets even *less* warmth or nurturing because parents and caregivers scold, yell, lecture or, sometimes, even hit. Then the cycle of feelings–behavior–punishment–behavior–punishment continues.

Over time, instead of learning how to express these feelings more directly in pretend play and words, the child tends to harden into a personality style that acts out, rather than communicates, feelings. Over time, the child may become less and less aware of the feelings that lead to the acting out. One reason we call this "constriction" is because a child's ability to experience fully all the feelings of childhood is reduced. The child's personality, in terms of her range of feelings and the thoughts and ideas that can be conceived, shrinks. Rather than a full and rich emotional life, the child has a narrow set of feelings and ideas and certain types of problem behavior that dominate.

The other aspect of this family's life that mirrors the experience of a growing segment of the American workforce is the necessity of meeting the challenges of working at home *and* trying to care for children. Usually, mothers undertake such challenges, but fathers can undertake them as well. The issues remain largely the same. John was imaginative and resourceful in his efforts and thus could inspire both mothers and fathers.

Even so, John skimped on playing with Gabriel when his business got hectic. He was good at comforting Gabriel and keeping excitement and other stresses from overwhelming him too much, but he kept cutting corners when it came to the wonderful smile-to-smile time. Eileen was right to encourage more of this type of sustained interaction, also called "floor time." As we've discussed before, this face-to-face interactive play is more than just fun. It's one of the best ways to help babies exercise their growing nervous systems and to master their most important new mental abilities. In floor-time play, babies learn to coordinate their senses—sights, sounds, smells—with their movements, all guided and orchestrated by their emotional interests, such as smiling back at you, reaching for something you're holding, and making funny sounds back when you make sounds at them. When we see parents or caregivers and their babies making noises and faces at each other, we're seeing babies falling in love and learning to be part of a relationship. As well, they're learning to be purposeful and to master their first lessons in cause-and-effect logic because they learn that a smile leads to a smile back. This interaction grows more complex as children become older. In the second year, a child learns how to solve problems by, for example, taking Daddy by the hand to find a favorite toy. All of this wonderful growth—physical, mental, and emotional—is accomplished through interactive play. It's fun, but it's also a crucial building block in children's growth as human beings.

Many parents who work at home under the pressure of phone calls, deadlines, and general exhaustion find it tempting to cut corners around this vital floor-time play. It's easy for such parents to recognize that a child needs to be fed and diapered, whereas the harm done by cutting corners on play is less obvious.

But, as we know, the fun stuff is where "the action" is. By shortening play time, hardworking at-home parents not only cut corners, they also cut opportunities for their child's growth.

This is particularly true for babies who seem content to be left on their own for hours at a time. It's easy for such "laid-back" babies to miss out on all the vital lessons described earlier because they seem so content on their own—gazing at shadows, playing with their feet—that parents are tempted just to let them be. Yet these are the babies who often need playful interactions the most.

Working at home can mean valuable opportunities to spend time with a baby, but it's also easy for work demands to undermine this very laudable goal. Working-at-home parents need not only to be disciplined about their work but also to protect their time with the baby. Since this is probably the reason parents are working at home in the first place, they should try to spend as much time as possible interacting and playing with the baby during his calm, alert, wakeful periods. As a general guideline, parents should aim to spend one half of a young baby's calm, alert time just with him. Before deciding that this goal sounds woefully unrealistic if you're trying to earn a living by working at home, keep in mind that these "calm, alert, wakeful" times can include diapering, feeding, bathing, and even burping. All these activities are opportunities for playful interactions.

A Four-Thirds Solution

When Elisabeth Schneider, a teacher, and her husband, Tim, a lobbyist, adopted their daughter, Katie, they didn't expect her arrival to affect their work lives much. But the Schneiders found themselves having to adjust to a life radically different from the one that they had envisioned.

Elisabeth and Tim's life turned upside down on a warm day in May when their two-year-old daughter awoke with a high fever. Elisabeth stayed home from work that day and the next, assuming that Katie had a virus that had been making the rounds of her daughter's day-care center. But Elisabeth grew increasingly worried as Katie's fever persisted. Katie seemed more thirsty than normal. Each day she drank quarts of juice and water and was urinating so frequently that Elisabeth had to change her diaper hourly. Katie, usually a smiling, sunny child, grew increasingly irritable and whiny. Tim was concerned as well, but Elisabeth, a chronic worrier, was worrying enough for the both of them. When Katie began vomiting, Elisabeth took her to the doctor, who ordered a urine test.

The tentative diagnosis: juvenile diabetes. It was a shock to both Tim and Elisabeth. The adoption files from the adoption agency appeared to have been meticulously maintained, and there was no mention of diabetes. But the doctor explained to them that it was entirely possible that Katie might have contracted diabetes through a virus that, for some reason, destroyed her pancreas's ability to make insulin, the hormone that regulates the metabolism of glucose. Until Katie was old enough to manage her diabetes by herself, Elisabeth and Tim realized, they were going to have to monitor her constantly. Her blood would need to be checked five times each day, and she would need insulin shots up to three times a day.

It was a frightening time for the family. Katie spent a week in the hospital while doctors stabilized her blood-sugar level and confirmed their initial diagnosis. Elisabeth and Tim struggled to get used to the idea that they would have to care for their daughter constantly and manage her disease effectively and safely. Through reading, they learned the devastating demands set by chronic childhood illnesses. Clearly, Katie couldn't continue to attend her day-care center while Elisabeth and Tim both worked; they feared the blood tests and insulin shots were too much for busy day-care center staffers to handle.

"You know what this means, don't you?" Elisabeth said to Tim in a panic. "She can't go to the day-care center every day."

"Well, I guess we'll have to hire a nanny," he said.

Elisabeth winced. The added expense was going to be painful. Tim worked for a nonprofit consumer organization, so he wasn't a very highly paid lobbyist, and Elisabeth's salary as a special education teacher in the public school system was fairly modest. Their bills were already high. Tim was paying child support to his ex-wife for their 16-year-old daughter. As well, Elisabeth and Tim were paying off a home-equity loan they had taken out in order to pay the $25,000 cost of adopting Katie.

"Nannies are unbelievably expensive," Elisabeth said.

Tim shrugged. "We'll just have to figure out a way," he said.

For days, the couple talked about the dilemma. Elisabeth took sick leave to stay at home with Katie while they figured out what to do next. Tim, who was more easygoing than Elisabeth, was less concerned about the outcome. He assumed that Elisabeth would figure something out. He quickly reabsorbed himself in his job after the obvious crisis was gone. He responded to Elisabeth's growing concern about caring for Katie while they both worked with a cheery wave of the hand. He said, "We'll figure out a way" so often that Elisabeth thought she was going to scream!

For the time being, Elisabeth threw herself into learning about diabetes. She joined a support group for parents of diabetic children. She took classes through the hospital and read books and magazines about the disease. She learned that coming medical innovations might eventually put an end to the constant blood-testing and shots, but until then, Katie's survival depended on constant monitoring and testing.

As for Katie, she disliked the constant blood-test pricking more than the actual shots. For a while, she disintegrated and screamed furiously every time she saw Elisabeth headed her way holding the blood-testing kits.

Elisabeth noticed that Tim seemed to be getting busier at work and was staying later for more business dinners or late meetings than usual. He even started going into the office on Saturday morning to catch up on paperwork.

Elisabeth wasn't particularly surprised by Tim's reaction to the latest development. He was a genial, outgoing man who simply wasn't good at dealing with bad news. In his first marriage, he'd been a fairly uninvolved father. He and Elisabeth had met while he was going through a divorce when his daughter was eight years old. Elisabeth noticed that he played "Disneyland dad" whenever he had his daughter—treating her to all sorts of presents and outings when she was with them on alternate weekends but then failing to telephone or stay in contact with her in between their weekends together. In fact, when Tim's ex-wife remarried and she and their daughter moved hundreds if miles away, Tim's contact with his daughter faded, although he faithfully paid his child support each month.

Tim hadn't been enthusiastic about adopting a child, but Elisabeth was determined to be a mother. Indeed, it had been a major issue between them even before they married. Tim felt he'd "been there, done that" when it came to parenting and wasn't very interested in joining the ranks of fatherhood again. Elisabeth, however, hadn't had her chance at it, and at the age of 40 she felt that biological motherhood was a long shot. Elisabeth, too, had been married previously, but that marriage had been so unhappy that children had been out of the question.

Once she met Tim, however, Elisabeth felt she'd found the "right" mate at last. As genial as Elisabeth was intense, Tim made her laugh and relax in ways she hadn't expected. After a long career of managing discount stores for a national chain, where she was desperately unhappy, Elisabeth went back to school at the age of 35 and got her teacher's degree. She enjoyed working as a special education teacher at an elementary school a short distance from their home. It was odd, she would think from time to time: as much as she worried and fretted in her private life, she seemed to have a lot of patience with rambunctious grade-schoolers.

In the end, Elisabeth won the baby debate, and the couple began the long process of adopting an infant from abroad. Katie arrived from China when she was four months old—a dark-haired baby with a warm smile who adjusted easily to her new life. Tim was relieved. He'd agreed to have another child mostly, he had to admit, to appease his wife. Elisabeth threw herself into caring for Katie, and Tim didn't have to change his life much. Elisabeth dropped Katie off at the day-care center in the morning and picked her up later in the afternoon after school got out. She was the one who took time off when Katie was sick and needed to go to the doctor's.

In the months after Katie's arrival, Tim gradually became more involved with her. He liked to play with Katie on Saturday mornings as she giggled and made believe that her teddy bear was eating his toast. Tim would pretend to gobble his toast up, while

Katie's teddy bear hunted for the toast in his pockets and down his shirt. Tim also took Katie to the park on Sunday mornings so Elisabeth could get some sleep, where he joked with the other dads as Katie clambered up the slide and toddled around with the other children.

So it was a particular shock to Tim when Katie's diabetes was diagnosed. Although he was normally upbeat and prided himself on "rolling with the punches," Tim was dejected by the news. He felt that by working hard and earning most of the money for Elisabeth and Katie, he'd basically done enough and deserved to come home from work and settle down in front of his computer. A nanny was the answer—expensive as it was.

Elisabeth, meanwhile, was exploring several options. She thought about quitting her job, but she loved teaching. She'd worked so hard to get where she was today that the idea of walking away from it all upset her deeply. But the idea of simply hiring a nanny seemed out of the question, financially and otherwise. Soon there would be college tuition for John's daughter; eventually there would be tuition for Katie's education too. Apart from the finances, Elisabeth worried about Katie's care.

"My sick leave is going to run out soon," Elisabeth told Tim one day when he came home even later than usual. "We really need to figure out our next step."

"Then let's get rolling and find a nanny as soon as possible," Tim said.

Elisabeth slowly shook her head. "That's not going to work," she said.

"Why not?" asked Tim. He was astonished.

Elisabeth tried to explain. "I just don't want to leave Katie with a stranger," she said. "What if something were to happen? How would we feel if something went wrong and we weren't there?"

Tim hadn't thought about that. He'd figured if they hired someone who was competent, she could handle things.

"Tim, there aren't any Mary Poppins out there," Elisabeth said. "Sometimes nannies are young, sometimes they don't speak English very well. And, besides, even if we found the perfect nanny, it still wouldn't be the same as if one of us were with Katie all the time."

Tim felt pained. He, too, didn't want to live without Elisabeth's paycheck, and it was clear that Elisabeth didn't think hiring a nanny was the solution.

"I don't think I'm up for shots and finger pricking," he said.

"I think you'll get used to it," Elisabeth told him gently.

Their talks did not lead to a solution, since neither Elisabeth nor Tim was willing to give up his or her work. As a short-term solution, they hired a nanny from a local nanny agency to care for Katie.

The nanny cost close to $500 a week, and Elisabeth and Tim realized they were fortunate that she wasn't more expensive in a high-cost area like the Washington, D.C., suburbs. She seemed competent enough, but Elisabeth was still worried. Was the nanny testing Elisabeth's blood enough each day? Was she playing with her enough? Elisabeth felt her heart race every morning when the alarm went off. Sometimes she felt it was tearing in two as she left for work in the morning.

It was Tim who unwittingly provided a solution to their dilemma. His organization was going through some downsizing, and Tim feared his job would be among the ones eliminated. When he came home with this news in mid-June, Elisabeth fought down the instinct to panic. They couldn't afford to survive on Elisabeth's salary. What would they do if Tim were laid off? Oh, calm down, she told herself. The economy is booming in this area. Tim can find another job quickly.

But what if he couldn't? she found she was asking herself. And then an idea began to take hold. What if he downsized himself and worked part-time for a while?

Elisabeth was excited about her plan, but Tim cut her short. He pointed out that they couldn't afford the mortgage on Elisabeth's salary.

"I know," said Elisabeth. "But here's the other part of my plan. Remember those people we met last year at that Christmas party? The two college professors who each worked reduced schedules while their children were little?"

"Yes, I think I remember them," Tim said slowly.

"Well, what if we tried something like that? Between us, we could take care of Katie most of the time, but still work."

"You mean both of us working part-time?" Tim asked. It seemed like a wildly impractical idea, yet at the same time, he found himself drawn to it. He wasn't entirely satisfied by his job, even though he had thoroughly absorbed himself in it.

For weeks, Tim and Elisabeth hammered out the details of their plan. Tim played devil's advocate, while Elisabeth tried to respond to his questions and objections with answers. It wasn't an easy process. They would need to sell their five-bedroom home and move into something smaller to bring their mortgage costs down. They would need to cut back on their expenses. Theater tickets and restaurant meals would need to be curtailed. But Tim gradually began to embrace the idea, although it also frightened him, he admitted to himself (but not Elisabeth). He approached his organization about cutting back to three days a week for a while. He wrote a memo to the group's executive director and followed up with a meeting. In order to make his proposal more palatable to his boss (whose wife was an at-home mother), Tim glossed over the fact that he would be doing this for the sake of Elisabeth and Katie. Instead, he emphasized that he wanted to take a kind of professional "sabbatical" for two years and also help the organization in their need to cut the budget.

Tim's boss was wary about the idea. Yes, the organization needed to cut back, and the reduction in Tim's salary would help, but he didn't like the idea of having someone who was "part-time," yet continued to receive health benefits, on the books. Despite his own doubts, Tim pushed ahead. He was intensely aware now of how much Katie needed the benefits, and how much Elisabeth loved her work. Tim had some long meetings with the director, in which they worked out the details, and Tim worked on resolving any doubts. The director feared that Tim could not keep up with the work in the three days he was in the office, but Tim pointed out that he has always been a hard worker and that he didn't expect that to change once he was working part-time. When the organization's board of directors finally gave their assent, Tim took a deep breath. Now comes the hard part, he thought.

Elisabeth, in the meantime, was also working hard to convince the higher-ups at her school that a suitable arrangement could be made. It was June, so Elisabeth hunted around to find another special education teacher who also wanted to work part-time. It wasn't hard to find a candidate! By word of mouth, Elisabeth found a teacher in a neighboring school who was expecting her first child shortly. She was reluctant to return to work full-time when school resumed. Together, the women wrote a proposal to share Elisabeth's job. They emphasized that the job sharing wouldn't cost the school system additional money (it helped that the other teacher was also using her husband's health benefits) and pointed out that they had worked out the details. Then they shopped the proposal to various elementary school principals and, finally, a principal bit. The school was a little farther away than Elisabeth would have wished, but she decided not to let that discourage her. Then they had to get approval from the school board to go from full-time to part-time. (Elisabeth wasn't sure why this was necessary, but she'd learned not to question a school bureaucracy's constant need for additional paperwork and approvals!) Elisabeth and Maria wrote another proposal to the school board, again emphasizing that their arrangement wouldn't cost any extra money and that they had a school principal who'd approved the arrangement, contingent on the school board's approval. They crossed their fingers as the board's monthly meeting rolled around—but their proposal easily won approval.

Selling their home turned out to be more difficult than Elisabeth or Tim had expected. Finally, however, they found a buyer and at the same time found a house to buy, settling on a townhouse that was a little closer to Elisabeth's new school.

In September, Tim and Elisabeth rolled out the new arrangement. Elisabeth worked Mondays, Tuesdays, and Wednesdays, and Tim worked Wednesdays, Thursday, and Fridays. They hired a babysitter for Wednesday morning until Elisabeth returned at three. Katie was now age three.

Elisabeth drilled Tim in the basics of caring for a diabetic child. Even so, the first time she left for her new job, she was filled with dread. What if Tim forgot to test Katie's blood? What if he failed to give her her insulin shot? What if her blood sugar dropped dangerously low? Would Tim think fast enough to grab the tube of cake frosting from the cupboard and squirt it in Katie's mouth so she would get some sugar in her system fast? Elisabeth had learned tricks like these from her diabetes support group, and she wished she'd been able to interest Tim in participating.

The first few weeks were difficult for Tim. The first time he pricked Katie's finger for a blood test, she screamed so loudly that he briefly considered taking her over to the school so Elisabeth could do it the next time.

Katie, also, wasn't used to so much time from Tim and, at first, she howled, "Want mommy! Want Rosie!" (her nanny) every time Tim approached her to test her finger or give her her shots. Tim retreated for a bit from this onslaught. He tried to read the paper and get some work done while Katie watched a "Blue's Clues" videotape.

Finally, Tim decided to take her to the park; he had visions of settling back in the warm sun and reading the newspaper while Katie scampered around.

Katie just stood there and whimpered.

"Go play, Katie," Tim insisted, but Katie began to cry instead. By the time they returned to the house, Tim was exhausted. After a snack and a check of Katie's blood sugar (she didn't scream so loudly this time), Tim put Katie down for a nap and settled down to rest himself.

"Want Mama!" he heard after only about 10 minutes. "Want Rosie!"

With a sigh, Tim heaved himself off the couch and went to Katie's room.

"Katie, it's nap time," he said. "Go to sleep."

But Katie was too upset. So Tim lay down on the floor of the family room and let Katie crawl all over him. She poked his stomach and sat on his chest and, giggling, tried to lift up an eyelid to see if he was asleep. To his surprise, he enjoyed this. Tim pretended to snore while Katie pretended to try to wake him up. She had great fun jiggling his legs, poking his stomach, and peering in his ears while Tim snored louder and louder. Finally, he opened his eyes wide and said, "Boo!" in a playful tone. Katie laughed so hard that she fell down, which made her laugh even harder.

Still, these weren't the easiest days of his life, and Tim often found himself wishing for the stability and rhythm of the workplace after a few hours with Katie. But he got through it. He discovered that Katie enjoyed physical play; she loved it when Tim pretended to stumble over a toy and then fell down, splaying his arms and legs out and opening his eyes and mouth. Katie giggled heartily and then showed him how she could fall down, too.

Gradually, Tim and Elisabeth's new schedule settled down. Elisabeth enjoyed being home with Katie during her days there. During Tim's days at home, Elisabeth at first felt continuously guilty about leaving him at home alone with Katie so much. She tried telephoning several times a day while she was at work to find out how things were going, but when she found that Tim seemed to be muddling through, she decided it was better to just let him phone if there were problems.

Tim had envisioned spending a lot of time in a comfortable chair in his home office, where he could send off e-mails on his computer and catch up on work. Although he liked roughhousing with Katie for a little while, he found her continual demands for pretend play tiring. He usually managed to find an excuse to end the game as quickly as possible. He'd look at his watch and decide it was time for another blood-sugar check or he would find a video for her to watch.

Tim also noticed, however, that as he and Katie found activities they could share, she seemed to get less upset about the finger pricks several times daily, which made the routine much easier for him.

Elisabeth also had her own challenges with Katie. When she came home on her workdays, Katie was often cranky and clingy. She would hang on to Elisabeth's legs. If Elisabeth managed to untangle herself and disappeared from her view even for a moment, she would scream hysterically.

Elisabeth alternated between feeling guilty and feeling frustrated by Katie's latest antics.

"I feel badly about leaving the two of you all alone," she told Tim. "I'd like to be calmer around her, but she's making me crazy because I can't get a moment to myself." Eventually she found that if she made time for a close reunion with Katie as soon as she got home, Katie would be less clingy later.

Bit by bit, the three of them eased into their new roles. Since Elisabeth was off during the summers, Tim and Elisabeth were able to bring in extra income during those months though freelance work. Elizabeth tutored some special education students during her "work" days during the summer, and Tim picked up some consulting work during some of the extra hours Elisabeth was at home. In this way, they were able to relieve some of the financial pressure they faced.

When Katie turned almost four and would enter a pre-kindergarten class in a few months, Elisabeth discovered to her delight that she was pregnant. After a few breathless days of "Oh my God, I'm too *old* to do this!" and "What do we do now?" Elisabeth and Tim decided to keep up their current arrangement.

———

There's plenty to be learned from the Schneiders' experiences. First, like many families, they put together a Four-Thirds Solution through trial and error. Child-care arrangements often evolve in this way, rather than according to a grand plan that couples put together in some systematic fashion. In the Schneiders' case, they felt they had no other choice.

In some ways, the Schneiders were fortunate. Katie was a warm, responsive child who was deeply and lovingly engaged with both her parents. She understood what people wanted from her by the look on their faces and by their slightest gestures, as well as through their words. She was a clear and organized communicator—logical and analytical as well as creative and spontaneous. She obviously enjoyed play and was assertive enough to compel her mother to become the partner she wanted. Katie flat-out demanded her fair share of pretend play. Her father, to his credit, gave it to her (though with some reluctance)! Katie was a flexible child, and this flexibility made it possible for her to deal with her diabetes better than most children.

A child who is this flexible and adaptable often is able to spend long hours in out-of-home child care without complaining or misbehaving in any way. Parents often assume that this means their child is doing fine in child care, even if it lasts as long as 10 to 12 hours a day. But such behavior can be misleading. Without the warmth and security that children get from at least a reasonable amount of direct parental care, it's difficult for them to develop emotionally and intellectually. Katie was fortunate. Her parents were forced to give her more care themselves because of her diabetes. Although the situation was challenging for Elisabeth and Tim, paradoxically, it was great for Katie because it brought her more time with her parents.

Elisabeth and Tim at times felt too controlled by their daughter and believed that, even though she was a sweet, bright, and creative little girl, she was too demanding. Their feelings of being overwhelmed in this situation are quite understandable, given the daily schedule they maintained and the meager breathing room that they had for themselves. At the same time, it's not surprising that Katie was sometimes clingy because she probably sensed her parents' subtle desire to escape every minute that they could.

Indeed, this clinginess can be a challenge for parents—particularly parents with demanding work schedules who feel they can least afford to have a child hanging on them constantly. But nothing makes a child cling more than the sense that "If I turn my back, Mommy or Daddy will be gone." In fact, the easiest way to turn around a clinging child is to take the initiative and offer the nurturing before she asks. For example, you can offer to play *before* your child asks, give big hugs and kisses more often than usual and let your *child* be the one to disengage from a hug or kiss. Sometimes all that is needed is to offer to take your child into the kitchen with you instead of just disappearing in there without telling your child where you are going.

This is a subtle aspect of relationships that most of us sense but rarely talk about. When you hug your spouse, who breaks off first? Do you sense your spouse is in a hurry? It is easy to sense when someone's mind is elsewhere or he or she is trying to move on to something more important. Your child feels much the same way if you are always breaking off hugs and kisses. Holding that hug a few extra seconds so that your child leaves you instead of *you* leaving your child can offer untold advantages. The child gains a confident outlook on life: "I have the security I need and therefore I can be the one to take the initiative" rather than "I have to hold on for dear life or someone will leave me!"

Hearing this, some parents may worry that they will spoil the child. The solution is to give more and, at the same time, *expect* more from your child. If, for example, you expect her to clean up her own toys or, when she gets older, to do her homework without constant supervision or show compassion and care for young siblings, then she learns independence, self-sufficiency, and assertiveness and as well gains a deep sense of security.

You can also help a child become more assertive. Show her how to ask for her juice rather than just bringing it to her when she whines that she's thirsty. Help her find her own toys rather than automatically fetching the doll or the ball yourself when she looks around for it. In pretend play, encourage her to play the wolf instead of always being the scared damsel in distress.

Taking the initiative in nurturing and encouraging assertiveness is a surefire way to reduce a child's clinginess. Tim and Elisabeth would benefit greatly from this approach.

Tim, especially, needs to work on these areas. Katie is not naturally close to her father, in part because he is a little more involved with himself than Elisabeth. Even though Tim is now spending more time with Katie, he has not yet really learned how to relax and be comfortable with the softer, playful, more intimate side of life.

I have high hopes for the Schneiders. They are a family with a great deal of love to go around. Elisabeth and Tim are tolerating a challenging schedule in the short run and concentrating on the important priorities in their lives. I'm sure they will find the balance they need. Their little girl's illness has forced them into an entirely new relationship with her and, hopefully, with themselves as well.

A special benefit of the Four-Thirds Solution is that it allows parents who are less comfortable with playful intimacy and more self-involved or more workaholic to learn how to enjoy their children. This can bring out an aspect of their personalities that they may not even know they had. Parents who are learning to be more playfully intimate with a child will discover rewards and pleasures far in excess of anything they ever imagined.

When we think of parents who aren't as involved with their children, we tend to think of fathers. But they're not the only ones who can benefit from the extra time for playful intimacy in today's busy world. Many mothers, too, find the organized, predictable world of work emotionally easier than the unpredictable, sometimes out-of-control world of child rearing.

In the past, at-home moms couldn't avoid coming to grips with the frustrations, annoyances, joys, and fulfillment of being an intimate part of their children's lives. Many fathers, however, could avoid such involvement if it was hard for them. Nowadays, both parents can hide behind demanding careers and miss an opportunity to become fuller and deeper human beings. In this regard, the Four-Thirds Solution is important not only for children, offering them intimacy and interaction with each parent, but also for parents, enabling them to move ahead in their *own* development. Like children, parents often need a societal push to help them jump into the uncharted waters of the emotional challenges that lie ahead. Whether it's a child who is going from hitting to talking or from playing all the time to doing schoolwork or whether it's an adult who is going from dependence on parents to leaving home and pursuing a career, individuals often need a push from society to get rolling!

Both men *and* women need new cultural expectations to enable them to become not only full "professionals" but also full "parents" in every sense of the word.

6

Choosing Child Care

For the hours when they cannot be with their children themselves, the challenge to parents is to find the best child care possible. Whether you choose a family provider who cares for your child in her home, a child-care center, a nanny, or a relative, keep in mind that your choice will have a great influence on your child's development. Contrary to what the term "baby-sitter" suggests—someone who just marks time with your child—this person (or these persons) will be like another parent during your child's most important formative years. As I discussed earlier, the capacity for intimacy and warmth, compassion and empathy, as well as the ability to communicate, think, reflect, and analyze develop as a result of the way our minds grow and establish vital foundations in the early years of life. From your child's point of view, choosing the right caregiver is a decision that is as important as picking your spouse.

Making the Choice

Although this may sound like a daunting task, in this chapter, I'll help identify the qualities in a caregiver that are likely to support a child's mental and emotional development as the child progresses from newborn to infant to toddler. These qualities relate directly to the six essential building blocks of emotional and intellectual development that I've described earlier.

Children need:

1. Safety, security, and a calm, yet interesting environment that will awaken their interest in sights, sounds, and other sensations.
2. Warm, nurturing, interactions with long-term caregivers, involving joyful feelings as well as sights, sounds, touches, and other sensations to foster learning, language, and attention.
3. Playful emotional interactions with long sequences of smiles and other facial expressions, sounds, and gestures.
4. "Discussions" without words—negotiations with gestures to solve problems.
5. Creative elaboration of ideas through pretend play.
6. Debates and discussions that elicit a child's opinions and foster logical thought.

When you read over these requirements, you may assume that I'm suggesting that only Ms. Perfection will do. Not so! It's important to remember that this is an *ideal*. You will never find a child-care provider who can completely foster your child's emotional and intellectual development in each and every one of these stages. Indeed, as parents, we probably can't either. For example, if you took an honest look at yourself as a parent, you might say, "I'm pretty nurturing, pretty secure and warm, but I really don't enjoy a lot of pretend play." Or "I can't stand endless debates!" The same goes for child-care providers. Most are not necessarily gifted in all these areas. For example, a child-care provider who loves pretend play—who will happily play Baby Bop to a child's Barney for hours whereas you know you would be dying of boredom—may not be as skilled at sparking logical interactions with a slightly older child. Our humanness and the compassion and caring that go with it is our most important caregiving quality.

Our humanness means we will not fit some mold of perfection. So as we discuss these desirable qualities in a caregiver, I'll talk about those that are essential as well as those that are assets but less essential. In short, you want a child-care provider who can help your child master as many of these stages of emotional development as possible. While you're interviewing or observing a child-care provider, there are key things to watch for, which I will discuss. Because this is such an important decision, *take your time.* Unfortunately, this decision is often made under great pressure. If a child-care provider quits or the day-care center closes down, parents are desperate to find a replacement because they fear missing work. But desperate situations breed bad decisions. That's when parents can end up hiring a provider who may be neglectful ("Oh, I thought I noticed that she hardly took any time to get to know my child, but I wasn't sure") or may select a poor-quality child-care center ("The center staff looked very distracted, but I just figured they'd had a busy day"). Later, parents realize that they saw the danger signals but didn't want to pay attention to them. They wanted it to be okay because they were so desperate.

It's obvious that any parent or provider who is taking the time to read this book loves his or her children dearly and wants the best child-care arrangement for them. Yet I've noticed that many parents display oddly paradoxical behavior when it comes to child care. While we may spend hours, days, even weeks, looking for just the right car or just the right sofa or just the right computer, we sometimes spend relatively little time looking for just the right child-care provider. We may be content with a couple of quick reference checks and a few moments of watching someone play with our child. Why is this? I suspect that it's both because of the perceived urgency and also because choosing child care is such an important decision that parents feel anxious. Sometimes we try to get over or deny anxiety by making a quick decision. Even taking a week, or more, off work in order to find just the right person or child-care center shouldn't be out of the question. Just as we wouldn't hesitate to take time off because our spouse or our mother was ill, similarly, we shouldn't feel that we are being selfish if we take time off to find the best caregivers for our babies.

Six Criteria for Quality Child Care

Now, let's walk through the six basic needs we've outlined to identify the kind of provider who is capable of filling them.

1. Safe Physical Surroundings and a Calm Yet Interesting Environment

First, the physical aspect. It should be fairly easy to find a child-care provider who provides for the physical safety of a child, as well as adequate food and the appropriate space for sleep and play. Unfortunately, however, we can't take even that for granted. Family day-care providers living in dangerous neighborhoods or in chaotic family circumstances may not be able to provide a safe, secure environment. You have only to look in the media to realize that too many family day-care homes and centers have safety hazards—from fire code violations to poor heating or cooling systems to peeling lead paint. So if you are seeking care outside your home, inspect the physical surroundings.

Make sure that the provider is state-licensed, while keeping in mind that possessing a state license doesn't automatically guar-

antee that a provider can be relied upon for the safety and security of your child. Most states have only minimal standards for
child-care providers. A review of state licensing standards for
child-care providers by the Commonwealth Foundation and Yale
University found that about two thirds of the states did not have
adequate regulations for child care and only one state got high
grades for its regulations. Some organizations concerned about
the quality of child care, such as the National Association for the
Education of Young Children and the National Association for
Family Child Care, offer accreditation programs. Accreditation
from groups like these is almost always helpful because it suggests that the provider is motivated and concerned enough to
seek accreditation. With that in mind, use your own judgment
and observe carefully and systematically the center or caregiver's
home carefully in terms of health and safety.

Next, try to determine the judgment of the individual caregivers, whether in a center or in a home. Can the nanny or family
child-care provider deal with an emergency? Does she speak
English well enough so that she can call the fire or police department? Does she have adequate knowledge of basic first aid? If it's
a center or family day-care home, do the people in responsible
positions have the training, background, and judgment to handle
a variety of medical or other emergencies.

Beyond the physical standards, babies also need an environment that will get them interested in the sights and sounds of the
world as well as help them be calm and regulated. Watch how
child-care providers play and interact with your baby and the
other babies in their care. Can they tailor their approaches to a
baby's individual needs? For example, are they soothing if a baby
appears overstimulated? Are they more animated if that's what a
baby seems to enjoy? Are they able to help a baby to look and smile
at them by the rhythm of their voices, by the way they hold her, or

by the distance between their faces and the baby's? Watch to see how they comfort a baby who gets irritable, colicky, or finicky.

There is no substitute for on-site observation. If you're in a big center with lots of child-care workers, find out who will be caring for your own baby and introduce yourself to her. If it's possible, ask her if she would like to get to know your baby. Watch her play with your child. Give her some pointers. ("She likes to have her toes tickled," or "She loves it when you get real close to her face and give her a big smile") and see how she responds. Watch how she holds and talks to babies and how she uses the information that you're giving her. Does she follow up on your suggestions, or does she ignore, or not appear to understand, them?

An environment that helps the babies learn to regulate themselves will not be too noisy and chaotic. Some centers place babies and toddlers in a large room together, with a low wall separating the two areas. But crying babies and busy toddlers can make for a very noisy environment. The same is true with a family child-care provider who is caring for several children in a small home. Bright lights, too, shining in a baby's eyes could overstimulate him. Listen and look for a few minutes and ask yourself whether you feel overwhelmed by the noise and sights. If you do, the chances are that your baby will, too. Similarly, see if a baby could feel neglected by or insufficiently involved with caring caregivers in this setting.

This aspect of child care—providing a child with secure surroundings and a calm yet interesting environment—is one that I consider essential. Every child needs such an environment.

Points to watch for

- A safe, secure environment (i.e., electrical outlets are covered, dangerous objects are out of reach, there is no peeling paint, stairways have gates).

- Providers with training to handle emergencies (CPR and first aid are a must).
- Quality of interactions with your baby and others: Do the caregivers' voices, facial expressions, and physical handling fit the needs of your baby?
- Caregivers' response to pointers on how to handle your child.
- State license.
- Certification from the National Association for the Education of Young Children or other organization accrediting early-childhood caregivers.

2. Caregivers Who Can Engage Warmly with Children and Treat Them with Loving Care

Babies need to fall in love with their caregivers and form a relationship with them in order to develop the ability to be warm, trusting, and intimate. Look for the child-care provider or providers who can foster joy and pleasure as well as a sense of comfort and security so that they can begin to form a warm, nourishing relationship. This is a much more intangible and hard-to-measure quality than safety. You want to find warmth and tenderness in a caregiver, someone who is engaging and emotionally nourishing to the baby or toddler.

There are three questions to ask in assessing whether the provider or providers you're choosing have these capacities: How does she relate to you? What is her background and experience? How does she interact with your child?

First of all, when talking to a potential nanny or family day-care provider, do you get a warm, pleasurable, comforting feeling? Do you feel comfortable with and sense her caring quality because of her voice tone, the way she makes eye contact, the way she smiles?

Or do you get an uneasy feeling, or a feeling of distance or aloofness. Does this person want to get close to you in an indiscriminate, gushy way that doesn't feel right? In the same way, observe the "scene" around you. What is your response to the overall atmosphere? Does the family day-care provider or do the child-care workers seem relaxed, warm, and caring as they go about their business or do they appear mechanical, stiff, or aloof? Do they appear anxious, frazzled, or disorganized? Pay attention to how you *feel* about the overall setting. You may sense the overall mood of a child-care provider's home or center, just as you can sense an overall emotional tone when you go into an office or a party—a sense of warmth coming from the group or a sense of rejection and coldness. Don't be afraid to use your intuition! Your gut sense of a person or place may tell you more than dozens of answers to factual questions (although those are also important).

Next comes the check into a person's or center's background. You are probably already aware of the importance of this step, but a surprising number of well-meaning parents do not follow through. They may feel too rushed, or they may find the child-care provider or center so appealing that they feel they don't need to take this step. But it's vital to take the time to check into backgrounds. You need a child-care provider who has experience with children who are the same age as your child and a little older. If you're hiring a nanny, ask her whether she has had experience with children who are your child's age. She may seem warm, sweet, joyful, and stable and have excellent references, but if she has no experience with children who are your child's age, she may not know how to handle them. For example, she may panic if a baby cries too much.

It is easy to have a criminal-background check run on an applicant, if you are hiring a nanny or family child-care provider. Many local private security firms will do this for less than $100, although you will need signed permission from the applicant. It is a very helpful step to take. For a child-care center, find out which department in your locality—it's usually the local Department of Social Services or the Department of Health—inspects child-care facilities and ask to see its file on the center you're interested in.

For individuals, get two or three references, including the person's last employer. Be ready to ask a number of the questions that we have been discussing.

You may be thinking about hiring an au pair. Usually, an agency brings au pairs in from Europe or elsewhere, and so you probably won't have a chance to meet with her personally. This situation calls for extra research and caution. Parents usually hire au pairs sight unseen, but they need to be wary. Before you consider handing over a baby or young child or even an older child to the care of an au pair, make *sure* she has had plenty of experience with babies and young children as well as older children. She needs to be familiar with the stress and challenges that caring for young children can bring. Perhaps she has young brothers or sisters or has had experience in caring for a neighbor's young children. Ask the agency for written or telephone references.

If you work in your home and need a part-time caregiver, you might be able to have someone who is not as experienced with babies, who will learn at first by being your helper. But if you work outside the home (and most working parents do), it's important that an au pair or any other caregiver have experience with babies. She needs to have a manner that is protective as well as warm and emotionally nourishing, and she needs to be comfortable dealing with the expectable demands and upsets of an expressive baby as well as know how to engage with a baby or child who may appear independent or self-sufficient.

When an au pair agency is making the choice for you, you need either to have enormous trust in the individuals who are making the decision for you or you need to make direct contact with your au pair, even over the telephone, to do your own explorations. If she lives in the United States, one parent may want to consider visiting her. If she lives in Europe, it still may be possible to meet her. If one of the parents does business abroad, he or she may be able to arrange to meet with the au pair personally before making a final decision.

If you're considering a child-care center, ask the employees who will be caring for your child about their experience with children the same age as your child. Ask them what kinds of challenges a child this age brings. It's easy to forget, when you're considering a center, that you need to interview the individual child-care workers who will care for your child, in addition to the manager of the center. Unfortunately, labor shortages have left child-care centers bereft of good job candidates, and even though they try hard, centers sometimes end up employing people who have little experience with children—particularly with babies. Ask them how they would handle a child like yours—for example, a child who cries a lot, or who is easily distracted, or who is very laid-back. If their answer is too glib or if they sound like they haven't had much experience with children, that tells you the person may not be qualified to care for your child.

Also, see if you can gauge whether the provider or center workers will be available for a lengthy period of time. As we've discussed, infants and babies ideally need the same child-care provider for the first three or four years of their lives. It helps them form relationships and from there, develop the capacity to be warm, trusting, and intimate with other people. A child whose caregivers change frequently will have less of an opportunity to form these lasting relationships.

Ask the center about their employee turnover and check with individual workers. How long have they been there? If most of them have been at that center for only a few months, it's a sign that your baby's caregivers may change more frequently than is ideal. Furthermore, most centers change babies' caregivers intentionally each year. For example, at many centers, babies move from the infant room to the young toddler room—and to a new teacher—at the age of 12 or 15 months. As we have discussed, it would be useful for day-care centers and parents to attempt to make the same caregivers available to children for longer time periods.

Ask about the training of the child-care workers. Does the center require a high school diploma, at least, or courses in child development? If you're considering a nanny or a family child-care provider, see if you can get a sense of what stage they are in life. Is the nanny a student who is working only temporarily? Does this person seem to be stable, with roots in the community, or is she rather isolated? Know her background, her relationships. What is going on in her family? Is it in a shambles or does she have a stable life with warmth and support? As you no doubt know, taking care of children requires a lot of emotional reserves. That's hard if your life is stressful and chaotic.

Finally, it is vital to observe the provider (or providers) interact with your child. Do they seem like people your baby would enjoy? Does your baby brighten up and smile and show some pleasure as they play together? Does the provider (or providers) seem emotionally distant or mechanical or does she seem overly intrusive and too eager? Does she appear depressed or withdrawn? How well does she woo your baby into a sense of engagement and relating? Even if you watch your baby with a provider for only 10 or 15 minutes, you can get a sense of how she might handle your child over a longer period of time.

Points to watch for

- Your intuitive reaction to the caregiver: Does she feel warm and intimate or aloof and distant?
- The overall feel of the child-care setting: Does the child-care setting have a warm, pleasurable feel or does it feel cold and mechanical?

- Background and experience: Do the providers have experience with children who are your child's age? What kind of training does the provider have?
- References: Get both written ones and the names of people to call.
- A personal visit or interview: With an au pair, at a minimum have some long phone conversations.
- Caregiver's way of interacting with your child: Observe them together in your home or at the center.

3. Communicative Caregivers Who Can Engage in Playful, Emotional Interactions

As we discussed earlier, babies and children need lots of communication with people nonverbally as well as verbally. They need to learn the all-important nonverbal cues—body language, gestures, and facial expressions—through which people communicate. With babies or toddlers, you want someone who will get down on the floor with them and play with them in ways that will help get this process cooking. With babies, the communication will be via smiles, head nods, giggles, laughter, vocalizations, annoyed looks, smirks, frowns. With toddlers, this nonverbal dialogue will continue, as lots of problem-solving negotiations such as finding a lost toy together take place, and verbal exchanges will be going on at the same time. Do the caregivers you're considering offer this kind of communication? Some caregivers are warm, nurturing, and loving but aren't inclined to interact with babies and children at this level. They may hold a baby on their shoulder, rocking and patting him in a warm and loving way, but they don't engage in a lot of interactive patterns. You don't see them, for example, playing peekaboo games or exchanging big smiles with your baby. With a caregiver who is skilled at this two-way communication, verbally as well as nonverbally, you may see an impish grin on her face, and an impish grin on your baby's face. They may exchange funny faces or they may play flirtatious little games, such as hide-and-seek with a rattle.

Here, too, you can use the questions we just discussed. How do the provider or providers relate to you? Does she communicate easily with your baby? Do you sense that she is playful and intimate or does she appear more standoffish? Also, when you check into the background and experience of nannies or family day-care providers, ask their previous employers or clients about how they played with the children. Ask the nanny or provider or person running the center whether he or she believes that babies and toddlers should be quiet? Or does the caregiver believe that babies and toddlers should be played with—giggling, smiling, flirting, and having a good time? You want a caregiver who will enjoy spending time engaged in these important two-way exchanges. See if the caregiver can do this in a range of situations. If the child is being assertive, does she still try to use two-way communication and gesturing, or does she withdraw and stop communicating? Does she try to reach out to a whiny, clinging child?

In other words, is this a setting that supports children's warmth and joyfulness, as well as their assertiveness, their (constructive) use of aggression, their empathy for others, and even their fear? You want a caregiver or caregivers who accept the full drama of human emotions—from fear to joy and everything in between. For instance, suppose in a day-care center a child is frightened—do the providers pause and offer a gentle back rub and talk to him about what scares him or help him play it out? Or is it a place where people just say, "Oh, don't be a sissy!" or "Come on, we don't have time for that now!" At the same time, children need an environment that sets limits for children who are impulsive or aggressive in a gentle but firm way so that there is a safe atmosphere for everyone. The best caregivers can set limits as if they were a big teddy bear—firm, gentle, but respectful—rather than by ridiculing children, being overly punitive, or by scaring them. I consider these skills critical to a child's development. Points to watch for.

- Dialogue: Is there communication going on?
- With babies: Is there an exchange of smiles and other facial expressions?
- With a toddler: Is there lots of back-and-forth preverbal conversation and problem solving that begin to include words, as well as animated facial expressions, vocalizations, gestures, and body language?

4. Caregivers Who Can Engage a Child in Long Sequences of Interactions or Long Dialogues in Which Problems Are Being Solved

Here, the emphasis is on *long* interactive sequences. You're looking to see if, in addition to being playfully interactive and exchanging lots of smiles, smirks, head nods, and the like, the caregiver enjoys long dialogues where the child has taken the initiative. For example, when a one-year-old reaches for a toy up on a shelf, instead of reaching up and efficiently getting the toy for him, does the caregiver take his hand and say, "Let's find that toy! Where could it be?" Eventually, of course, they find the toy, but the point of the little game is to help a child learn to communicate back and forth with someone for longer periods of time. Obviously, you don't need a caregiver who does this precise sequence! And she can't do this all the time—nor should you expect her to. But you do want someone who is willing to engage in conversations (gestural and sometimes with a few words) in which a "problem" is being solved. These interactions foster early types of thinking and social skills. In a busy child-care center where there may be one caregiver caring for six or eight young toddlers, it can be quite difficult to engage in these long "problem-solving" dialogues. Older children, two-year-olds and above, are often able to engage each other in these long dialogues, but younger children are not able to. For this reason, it's crucial that you have child-care workers who can provide these opportunities.

Points to watch for

- Conversations: Watch to see whether caregivers are able to communicate verbally as well as nonverbally to babies and young children for long periods of time.
- Playful games: Look for the little signs. If your child announces that he wants to go outside, is the nanny the kind of person who simply puts his coat on and leads him to the door, or does she offer him her hand and say, "Can you show me where you want to go?"
- Questions for the child: When a child is beginning to learn some words, does the caregiver ask him what he wants to do outside or does she just take him out there without any discussion?

5. A Caregiver Who Can Help a Child Learn to Use Ideas

As you may recall, this skill begins to emerge when a child is about 18 months old. Children begin to build their inner world of ideas, which is the fuel for their future creativity and helps them build a sense of who they are as people. They do this by learning to form mental pictures or images—to form ideas about their wants, needs, and emotions. A child who says, "Want pencil," instead of just grabbing it is using ideas or symbols, as is the child who says, "Give me that," or "I'm happy," or "I am mad" instead of taking an action (grabbing, kicking, or hitting). Adults can help children learn this important emotional skill in two ways: through pretend play with a child or between the child and other children, and by enjoying long verbal dialogues with the child. Some adults like to give instructions to children and expect them to obey. Other adults like children to be quiet. Neither adult is going to help children build a world of ideas.

Talk to the child-care provider you're interviewing and, first, check out whether she is able to have a fairly involved conversation with you. Ask about her background and what she talks about with the children she has cared for. What is her philosophy about children? For example, does she like to see a child express himself? You want to avoid caregivers who believe children should be "seen and not heard"! When you watch her play with your child or other children in a center, does she enjoy communicating with the children? Some people deal with adults and children very differently, so even if you are impressed by what a caregiver says to you, see if you notice anything different when she is dealing with children. Of course, anyone in this situation is going to be on her best behavior. But if she appears to prefer simply sitting there while the children crawl over her, or if she tries to ignore the children until they are very persistent, that tells you something. Does she seem to enjoy children's imaginative play? Does she willingly become the dragon that your three-year-old "soldier" decided he wants to do battle with? Do you see providers at a center participating in tea parties with the teddy bear or "playing house"?

Points to watch for

- Conversation with you: Does it have much give-and-take?

- Conversation with a child: Does the caregiver get included in imaginative play or long dialogues?
- The caregiver's focus: Does she talk to her coworkers all the time, or does she get down on the floor to play with the children?

6. A Caregiver Who Can Be Rational and Logical, and Who Enjoys Hearing Children's Opinions and Debating with Them

In this stage, as you may recall, children go beyond just labeling a feeling—they gain the ability to *think* with these images. Between the ages of about two and a half and four, children learn to make connections between different ideas and feelings: "I am mad because you didn't play with me," or "I happy because Mommy home." It's a rather sophisticated ability. It means connecting two feelings or ideas across time and recognizing that one is causing the other.

We see this in their make-believe play. Children start to develop plots in their make-believe games—one set of ideas and another set of ideas become connected up. For example, a child's Pokemon will fight, not just randomly, but for a cause. This ability to build bridges between ideas underlies all future logical thought.

At this stage, children begin to make the distinction between fantasy—things that are inside "me"—and reality—things that are outside "me." Eventually, they are able to use this distinction to control their impulses and to concentrate and plan for the future. "If I do something bad to someone else, I may hurt the other person, and I may get punished." They begin to understand that the world works in this logical way.

By playing and interacting with children, caregivers and parents have a big role in the development of these skills. You need someone who is willing, even eager, to have lots of conversations with your child to help bridge his own ideas and to help him bridge his ideas to *her* ideas. The skill we were talking about a few pages earlier focused on the caregivers' ability to enjoy the world of ideas through pretend play and conversation. Now we're looking for the caregiver who is not only able to enjoy pretending and conversation, but one who can help a child make sense of his ideas. For example, when a child rambles on about a green bear, then a blue car, a caregiver can help the child build a bridge between the two. She could say, for example, "I'm lost. How did we get from a green bear to a blue car?" The child might then rise to the challenge and say, "Oh, the green bear is going to go for a ride in the blue car!" In this way, preschoolers learn to be both imaginative and logical. A caregiver who can help "build bridges" like this will talk to your child about the playground and friends so that he gets better and better at holding a logical conversation. Caregivers who jump from one subject to another and don't try to follow up on ideas have a hard time helping children master this new milestone.

All of this may sound terribly complicated and sophisticated, and you may be tempted to throw up your hands, convinced that you'll never find anyone skilled enough to raise children in a healthy manner. (In fact, you may think at this point that *you* don't have the skills yourself to raise you child in a healthy manner!)

But what these criteria come down to is a caregiver who is willing, even eager, to engage with children. She likes to hear a child's opinions. This helps children reflect on what they want to do and why, rather than simply getting what they want. It's probably something that you often do automatically at home. When a child says he wants to watch TV, you may ask him, "Why? What do you want to watch?" Or if he's choosing between an apple and a cupcake for snack, you may have a short conversation with him about which is better. This doesn't mean either giving in or getting your way. It means helping the child learn to reflect on what she wants or wants to do. You want a caregiver who is willing to discuss things with your child, not just give orders or give the child what she wants.

Points to watch for

- Listening: Does a caregiver exchange ideas, or get the child's opinions?
- Discussions: Does she seem to enjoy talking with a child about a variety of subjects?
- Allowing debate: Is the caregiver willing to negotiate and give the child reasons why, for example, he can't throw the ball in the house or wear his muddy boots inside? Or does she appear to expect to be instantly obeyed with no questions asked?

Working with Your Child-Care Provider

As I noted at the beginning of this chapter, all of these qualities together make up the *ideal*. No child-care provider has all of them, and neither does any parent! But when you're looking for a child-care provider, you want someone who has at least some of these qualities. I consider certain of the qualities to be nonnegotiable. A child-care provider who provides a safe, secure, calm environment is a must. I'm sure almost all parents would agree with that. A child also must have a caregiver who is nurturing and can bring a sense of joyful relatedness to a relationship with a child. I also think that a caregiver who is communicative and playful is a must.

If your caregiver speaks little English, she can still excel at providing safety and security, warm nurturing, playful interaction, and gestural as well as partially verbal communication. In fact, with a baby or toddler, it's better for the caregiver to communicate in the language she is most comfortable in because the preverbal child responds more to facial expressions and vocal rhythms as communicators of emotions than to the meanings of words. I would rather have a child hear natural rhythms and the emotional expression of a native tongue, plus pick up some foreign language skills, than have a foreign-born child-care provider try to communicate in English, where her expression of ideas would be limited and less natural.

At the higher levels of fostering creative play and thinking, as well as fostering analytical reasoning, there are enormous differences in people's abilities, and we need to be realistic. Try to figure out what you are good at and get a sense of what your caregiver is good at. See if you and the caregiver complement each other. You can each fill in what the other misses. If you have a child-care provider who isn't so strong in fostering logical thinking, who just isn't comfortable engaging in little debates with your child throughout the day, you can fill in the gaps. You can make sure that a child gets practice with these kinds of interactions when you're with her.

We can't expect caregivers to be perfect, any more than we expect to be perfect ourselves. When it comes to providing a safe, secure, warm, loving environment with a caregiver or caregivers who are playfully interactive, we *can't* compromise. On the other levels, find a caregiver who comes as close as possible, and then fill in the gaps—just as, you'll probably discover, a caregiver will fill in some of *your* gaps. If your caregiver is not as gifted at pretend play, using ideas, or building bridges between ideas, then parents can more easily make up for this in evenings and on weekends.

Once you hire someone, give yourself a chance to monitor how things are going. Just pop in unexpectedly. You can simply tell the child-care provider that you need to bring your child something or need to give them some information about your child. In those unexpected visits, come in quietly and try to observe for a few minutes. What's going on? What is the atmosphere like? Try to look for some things we've talked about in this chapter. Keep the "tips" in mind and look for them when your provider and child are busy with their day.

A growing number of child-care centers are installing surveillance cameras so parents can check in on their children over the Internet on their computers at work. Some parents even use these in their homes. Miniature ones can be hidden in a book or plant so you can observe your nanny without her knowledge. Many companies now sell or rent these devices.

Such devices imply a level of distrust that may not make for a good relationship. I prefer the old-fashioned system—dropping in frequently and at different times of the day. A caregiver should learn to expect to see you at any time. She shouldn't feel offended when a parent drops by. In fact, be very wary of a provider or a center that discourages drop-in visits, or of a family provider who insists that you drop off and pick up your child only at the front door.

It is also important that your child-care provider be willing to *collaborate* with you. She should be willing to work with you as part of a team, to share information with you about your child, tell you about his good days and bad days, and be interested to hear about your child's nights and weekends. She shouldn't appear to be possessive of a child or competitive with parents, with an attitude of "I know better." She needs to be empathetic to your relationship with your child. Is she able to be thoughtful and reflective about the difficult times your child has—for example, when he is being defiant, or aggressive? It's helpful when a child-care provider can talk calmly about these occasions, rather than react with exasperation or frustration when you try to discuss various incidents. This will give the two of you an opportunity to try to support one another and try to figure out what's really going on. (Naturally, you need to be thoughtful and reflective as well!)

Children who are learning a new skill—walking, playing with peers, riding a bicycle—need some help over these hurdles. Try to discuss these challenges with the caregiver. Explain that the child may need extra nurturing as well as opportunities to talk about their fears (if they're old enough), or opportunities to explore the challenge through pretend play. Children often need time to practice these skills. Also, make sure that you and the caregiver are aware of these challenges so you can both work on them with your child. There are many child-care providers who are very knowledgeable and gifted with children. They will lead and teach parents about many of the points raised in this chapter. When this is the case, parents can learn a great deal from their child-care provider. In general, the goal should be working together and learning from each other.

It's hard to entrust your child's health, intelligence, and emotional well-being to another person or people. But having a warm, empathetic relationship with their child-care provider or center benefits everyone—you, the caregivers, and, most important, your child. With that kind of a relationship, you can both feel comfortable sharing ideas, tips, and observations that help both of you nurture your child's healthy development.

PART THREE

Where Do We Go from Here?

7

Solutions for Families and Communities

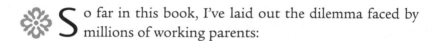 S o far in this book, I've laid out the dilemma faced by millions of working parents:

- Who will care for their children while they are at work?
- Can those caregivers provide what children need in order to become intelligent, morally sound adults who will be loving, compassionate members of society?
- In broad terms, can parents meet the basic needs of children while pursuing a career and engaging in other family relationships?

But, as virtually all working parents realizes as they race through their workweek—battling traffic to and from day care, negotiating with a spouse over who stays home with a sick child this time, dealing with a boss who thinks employees should leave their family life behind while at work—they *can't* do it all.

Urgent changes are needed—in family roles, in day care, in laws and governmental regulations, in corporate policies—before we can truly say we've done our best for future generations. In the following chapters, we will look at some of the needed changes in each area.

Pressures on Families

The families that we have discussed in this book have struggled to work out their own private solutions. Each would have found this easier had they been supported by a culture that placed greater value on the experiences that promote healthy growth and development in children.

Our modern world has brought us much-needed changes in some aspects of family life, such as increased equality of the sexes. But it has also put great strain on the family. Forces never even imagined in more distant times are prying us apart in ways we never could have foreseen. Family members often live long distances from each other. Many children have grown accustomed to seeing their grandparents and other members of their extended families only a few times a year. Urban sprawl contributes to long hours of commuting. Long work hours can make family meals rare.

In all these ways, we have redefined the role of the family in our society. Family members are seen as much less crucial to our everyday lives than in the past. As we have discussed at length in this book, we are farming out care of our children to others and accepting the fact that more than half of the young children in this country, perhaps even more in the future, will spend most of their time in the care of nonfamily members. It is important that we understand the consequences.

Some may argue that there have always been large sections of the human population off on their own tangents, in ways that don't result in healthy children. But as long as a significant portion of the population is being raised with sound nurturing, society as we know it and need it will survive. If, instead, we are putting millions of children in danger of losing nurturing aspects of human nature, we face the very real prospect of leaving ourselves bereft of the critical mass of emotionally and intellectually healthy individuals needed to run any society.

If our need for closeness to other humans, our sense of family, and our sense of community is stretched beyond a certain point, as a society and as individuals we should be experiencing these changes as painful. I believe that, in fact, these bonds are indeed being stretched so far that we *are* experiencing significant pain, although we may not recognize its cause. Some worrisome signs are the high rates of violence and suicide among our young people. The United States has one of the highest rates of youth violence of anywhere in the world. Incidence of drug abuse, divorce, and mental illness are also high in relation to other developed nations.[1]

Statistics on crime, drug use, depression, suicide, and so on are crude indicators of what's happening to our society. We also need to look at more subtle symptoms—such as the quality of impersonality in our everyday lives. Many feel that our national character has slowly but steadily grown more narcissistic and self-interested, more devoted to materialism. In an earlier book, *The Growth of the Mind*,[2] I traced these changes in mental health, education, family relations, and politics.

Perhaps the most telling symptom of our collective denial is to deny our own babies' need for us. Most who read this book would no doubt argue that, of course, we know that babies need their parents, and yet, we have to ask ourselves some hard questions: Are we *really acting* as if babies need their parents when close to 50 percent of babies spend the greater part of the week without contact with either parent? Does a few hours in the evening really acknowledge the deep yearnings we believe babies have for their mothers and fathers? The denial of our needs for intimacy need no further evidence than this striking and growing trend of farming out the care of those we love the most to individuals we hardly know.

In all walks of our modern lives, a weakening of the emotional relationships that sustain us in the workplace as well as in our other community relationships leaves all of us with a constant sense of unease or insecurity. Many survive by denying the very need for constant, secure, satisfying relationships, much like young adults who've been hurt in their love relationships and decide to play the field and simply enjoy casual sexual flings. The underlying need for more ongoing and more stable sources of intimacy doesn't disappear. It's denied, and opposing values are put in place to maintain the denial.

Something as basic as our need for intimacy and stable relationships can't successfully be denied forever, however, and invariably, this unfilled need has an effect on us. Once we deny the need for dependency and intimacy in ourselves, it's not surprising that we need to deny it in our children. To focus on their need for us, not just for an hour or two in the evening but throughout the day during the early years of life, would put us face to face with our own yearnings both for our children and for the other relationships in our families, in our community, in our workplaces that have the potential to sustain us in a more deeply human manner than we are currently experiencing.

A New Family Ethic

From the point of view of the family, we need to push aside this denial and create an ethic in which relationships—between parents and their children, between parents themselves, among members of extended families, and between families and their communities—begin taking a more dominant role. This ethic need not be a particular political philosophy. It would respect flexibility, freedom of choice, and gender equality. It wouldn't be a particular prescription for the family, but a move toward valuing the underlying emotional relationships that constitute family and community.

How does a "new family ethic" translate into everyday life? It does not mean that parents stop striving for a better material and cultural life for their families—obtaining better housing, moving to neighborhoods with better schools. But the emotional nurturing that children need should be seen as just as important as these. If this means staying in a school district with less-than-perfect public schools rather than stretching so far financially to afford a home in an area with better schools that both parents must work full time, then staying put may be the better choice. Life is always going to be a series of difficult decisions and balancing of needs—but in the early years of children's lives, their needs must be put first. Such an ethic would have the following basic features:

1. Job Schedules Structured So That Children Come Before Work

Parents need to look hard at their financial situation and their work schedules and create more time for their children. In the early years, this means that children spend most of their time with one or the other parent. As shown in Chapter 5, this may require a rather radical restructuring of schedules. For some families, it will mean a change in lifestyle. The necessity of expensive cars, large homes, fancy furniture and clothing, pricey tutors, extracurricular activities, and pricey summer camps for children, and the other trappings of an affluent modern family must be reexamined. Are they being obtained at the high price of less time with the children?

Even if parents choose to send one parent into the workplace while the other stays home with the children, that doesn't mean that the parent working outside the home must sacrifice family time to a career. For example, a parent with a heavy workload can come home for dinner and after-dinner family time, going back to work after the children are in bed. Children need the involvement of both parents, even if one parent is spending more time with them than the other.

If both parents need or want to maintain careers, the Four-Thirds Solution and the others shown in Chapter 5 are possible options. Small children, as we have discussed, need the care of their own parents for at least two thirds of the workweek. There is a huge difference between a child who spends one third of his week or one third of each day in child care, and a child who spends all day every day in child care. The basic premise of the Four-Thirds Solution is that children's needs must be the chief concern in both parents' career and financial decisions. Parents can supply the two thirds of direct parental care in many different ways.

What of single parents? Obviously, they don't have a choice of working or not working. The same goes for parents who are struggling financially with two low-paying jobs. In such situations parents can only do their best, keeping in mind that any family time, no matter how brief, is very important. They'll need to use their creativity and ingenuity. For example, they can turn dinner-preparation time into family time by including the children in the work, instead of letting them sit in front of the TV set.

2. Ongoing, Nurturing Relationships Within the Family

This means spending time with children, not just being in the same house. An adult family member needs to be available to babies for two thirds of the their waking time (sleeping time doesn't count!). And of that waking time, parents should spend two thirds of it divided between direct interaction with the child (playing with the child, feeding the child, changing diapers) and indirect facilitation of what the child is doing. For example, while cooking with the preschooler "cooking" nearby, you can talk about your special food. Translated into hours, that means if a baby is sleeping 11 to 12 hours a day, an adult family member needs to be with the baby between 8 to 9 of the remaining 12 to 13 hours. Close to two thirds of that time (about 5 to 6 hours) should be spent in direct and indirect interaction with the baby.

It isn't as daunting as it seems when you think of how much time you spend feeding, diapering, and otherwise caring physically for a child and when you consider that, for part of the day, there are two adults available to the children.

As children grow and sleep less, the time a parent needs to spend with them will increase slightly, but when children get to grade school, the time decreases, since they'll spend at least six hours of their day in school. When children get older, they don't require the hours-long attention from the adults in their lives as they did when they were babies and toddlers. In the case of grade-school children, parents should strive to spend two thirds of the time after school and peer play with their child to maintain that warm, nurturing relationship they have worked so hard to build. Grade-school children may spend some time in an after-school activity and playing with peers, but at least one parent should aim to be home by the time the child is home, with both parents available most of the time after dinner.

One last observation here: I've noticed through my practice that a lot of busy parents drift into a kind of "special treat" family existence, where they have little time with their children during the week but try to make it up on weekends or with occasional adventures, such as trips to a ski resort if the family is affluent, or with periodic vacations. But this only-the-icing-on-the-cake approach to family life means parents are not offering their children day-to-day nurturing and attention—the meat-and-potatoes that children need on a daily basis. Occasional trips or special weekend excursions can't make up for weekday work schedules that bring mothers and fathers home at 8 or 9 P.M., too exhausted to do much more than kiss children good night and put them to bed.

3. Opportunities for Developmentally Appropriate Emotional and Intellectual Interactions

One of the best ways to achieve this goal is through what I call "floor time." Floor time is a special period—at least 30 minutes a day—which you set aside for yourself and your child. During that time, you try to follow your child's lead as you play. This is a period when your child is in charge. The goal is to "march to your child's drummer" and to tune into your child at his level. With younger children, you literally get down on the floor to play. With older children, you may hang out in their room talking or maybe play basketball. Floor time goes beyond the idea of "quality time" because the child determines the direction of the play or conversation. Passive activities, such as doing a puzzle for a child or reading a book to a child or even watching an educational TV show with your child (instructive and important as they are) do not count as floor time. You need to be fully involved. Turn off the TV, turn down the stereo so that nothing distracts you from interacting with your child. The exchanges between the two of you don't have to be deep or even about the events of the day. You are simply tuning in and becoming part of your child's world. You are warm, empathetic, and open to what the child wants to do or say. The precise words you use aren't as important as the mere fact that you are, at least symbolically, down on the floor with your children. The very process of floor time conveys to your child that he is valuable and lovable, gives him a sense of being cared for, of feeling loved and secure and understood.[3]

These interactions with children will also include limit setting and guidance. Firm rules, discussions of rules, problem solving to anticipate difficult situations, and learning to deal with frustration are all part of this guidance. Discipline from involved, loving parents leads toward the ultimate goal of self-discipline.

4. Involvement in Children's Schools and Community

Children need to see that their parents are not only doing their best to provide them with warmth, protection, and security but also are extending those efforts out into their schools and communities. Children feel more secure when they see that the adults in their lives are working together for their protection and growth. At the school level, parents need to stay in touch with their children's teachers and try to volunteer a few hours a week in their child's classroom or in other ways that would help the school. They also need to learn about the governance and values of their children's schools by attending PTA or school board meetings. Together, parents and children can get involved in the religious institutions in their communities such as churches, synagogues, and mosques. Parents' involvement doesn't need to be time-consuming or complicated. It can be lobbying for speed bumps in the neighborhood to slow traffic or serving on the board of the community pool. In neighborhoods where there is inadequate protection from physical violence because of crime and drug use, parents can organize to accompany children to and from schools, and meet with local law enforcement officials and others to lobby for better protection. Parents can demand better, safer learning environments for their children from local school officials. Such involvement can yield big benefits to children. Even if parents make only slight progress toward these goals, there is an enormous increase in a child's sense of connection and belonging when they see parents working in community efforts on their behalf.

5. Cultural and Family Continuity

Providing a sense of cultural and historical continuity for children is also important. Encouraging children to have close relationships with grandparents and extended families is a wonderful way to achieve this. Exploring books, museums, and family birthplaces together can help them develop a pride in their cultural heritage.

Community Support

If we expect our children to develop the social ties that enable them to function as members of families and communities, then we need to focus on constructing communities that will help them do that. Our communities function well and thrive for the same reasons that permit families to function and thrive—the human ties between us. Groups of individuals, whether they are in families, towns, suburbs, or big cities, are governed by certain rules and regulations. These, in turn, survive only through the individuals who implement them. For example, a jury of 12 individuals must be willing to serve to interpret the law on a particular criminal or civil case. This all comes down to the way humans coalesce, or don't coalesce, into working groups that constitute families and communities. Rules and laws may be able to create a legal structure, but it takes the cohesive functioning of groups of individuals to put this to work.

In order for families to carry out the responsibilities we have outlined, they need the support of a larger community. Communities must become an extension of the family and effectively provide functions that the family can't provide for itself—safety, health, and social services in times of need, support for children, education, and recreation. Rather than think of our community structures as faceless bureaucratic bulwarks built around the maintenance of parks and roads, providing police and fire protection, maintaining libraries, and providing social services, we need to think about the degree to which the community supports the crucial family relationships that we have been exploring in this book. That means drawing more people into participating in the community structure, so that ultimately communities are an expression not just of the will of the government but also the needs of the governed. Instead, what we see happening in many local jurisdictions (as well as on the national and international level) is the creeping impersonality in public community life that we're seeing in families. We see an increasing sense of disenfranchisement of citizens vis-à-vis the bureaucratic edifices that they are supposed to be empowering. This trend must be countered. Some concrete suggestions for doing this include:

Revamp existing community centers and build more of them—particularly in communities where churches and social organizations are not as strong and healthy as they need to be.

These centers could function almost like extended families in communities without strong familial links between and among citizens. After-school activities, educational programs for people trying to get a high school diploma, first-aid classes, games, and lectures could all take place there. Such activities, after all, are part of the glue that holds communities together. These centers need to be decentralized and small enough for people to get to know one another. A city needs a number of different neighborhood centers.

Expand the use of our school buildings.

Schools can become extensions of community centers and even replace them in neighborhoods without any such centers and without the resources to build them. Schools should be open throughout the afternoon and evening as long as the community has a use for them. Midnight basketball for the youth in a community, community meetings, political meetings, a wide variety of classes are among the possible needs of a neighborhood that could be met by an existing school building.

Give a personal face to other community structures.

Government organizations such as police forces, boards of education, and social service agencies are often seen as burdens on families, rather than as invaluable aids. Indeed, sometimes these organizations seem to see families as the enemy—the dysfunctional source of domestic violence, or of interfering parents who won't let the schools do their job, and so on. But we need to modify that view of families. If we want to pull children back into the circle of care in our communities, we need to see them as part of a larger circle in society. When the agencies and organizations that serve a community can see supporting families as a goal, the whole community benefits. Families, too, need to change their view of these organizations, and see them as allies and resources.

Hospitals, clinics, and emergency rooms, which are often the places where the results of child and spousal abuse first become apparent, could be the focus of positive innovations for greater community integration. These need to be staffed with "family-support" teams that can intervene early and effectively to work with troubled families. These teams could also work with parents who just need some education in, say, removing in-home dangers from children's way.

Day-care centers also need to be integrated more fully into our communities. These are often where the effects of family stress can be seen first, for example, a parent who is always late to pick up a child or who looks tired and depressed each morning, or a child coming in hungry and tired each day.

Even neighborhood taverns and bars can, through community outreach, be pulled into a network where potential problems can be identified and dealt with—for example, a bartender might encourage a regular customer with some personal difficulties to see "a friend" at the neighborhood community center who happens to be a social worker—or where an emergency telephone number can be called for a customer who needs to be helped home safely. The same structure would be present at the local country club or the pool or the local tennis courts. In other words, we need, deliberately and methodically, to build an informal as well as formal support infrastructure much like that in the ideal of a small town, where everyone knows everyone and where people look out for one another, especially the children.

8

Improving Day Care

M any families need to rely, to varying degrees, on different types of day care for their babies and young children. Therefore, it is vital to improve the quality of day care as much as possible.

In earlier chapters, we've talked about the importance to children's development of having a consistent, loving caregiver or caregivers who provide interactions for the child geared to his changing developmental levels and needs, and also to his individual differences (i.e., how he reacts and takes in information and organizes responses). All children need to have these needs met, whether they are in day care or at home.

Consistency of Care

A first goal in improving day care is to foster more consistency in the caregiving available in day-care centers, as well as deeper levels of intimacy and security. What factors foster these attributes? Perhaps the most important is to help caregivers find meaning in the relationships they have with the children they care for. To accomplish this, we need to reduce the number of babies and children each caregiver has charge of. It's very difficult for a single caregiver to care for four infants, yet this is the norm in most child-care centers. Even twins are enough to exhaust the hardiest moms! Therefore, caregivers should be required to care for no more than three babies at any one time. Babies require relationships of continuing intimacy that are very difficult to provide if a caregiver is caring for four babies at a time. For toddlers in their second year, there should be no more than four children to one adult. For two- and three-year-olds, ideally there should be no more than five children for each caregiver; the maximum would be eight.

If we can succeed at providing the depth and intimacy and nurturance that infants and children require, we then must attempt to provide this in a consistent manner over a long period of time. This means that ideally, the same caregiver is with that baby during the first three to four years of life. When a baby is spending 35-plus hours a week in day care, the baby's relationship with a caregiver will be almost as important as her relationship with her own mother and father. Losing such a person after six months—because of job turnover or at the end of the first year because rules of the day-care center dictate that a baby must graduate from the baby room into the toddler room—is not what any of us would prescribe for a baby trying to grow emotionally in a healthy way. Would we deliberately recommend changing mothers every year?

As I mentioned earlier, a number of day-care providers have confided to me that in anticipation of losing a baby at the end of the first year, they "try not to get too involved," because it would be too painful when the baby moves on. For these reasons, we need to urge day-care centers to change their policies and administrative structures so that the same caregivers can follow a group of babies for three or four years, rather than have the babies move on every year.

Improve Caregivers' Wages

To create incentives for caregivers to provide intimate care and stay with their jobs for longer periods of time, we need to find ways to improve the wages of day-care providers. We can't give people the most important responsibility on earth—nurturing a baby—and pay them the most minimal wage possible. If we do, we can expect that competent individuals will look for better jobs paying higher wages—which is exactly what has been happening for the last several years as the American economy boomed. We need to restructure caregivers' wage scale to begin on a higher level so that more and more talented individuals compete for these important jobs. An escalating wage structure, as exists in some schools for master educators, is also essential if experience and talent are to be rewarded. A number of states have begun funding programs in recent years to reward child-care providers with pay raises and bonuses if they seek education and training. In California, some child-care providers can earn up to $6,000 in bonuses and extra pay in a year.[1] Other states' programs are more modest, and these programs need to be expanded to offer more compensation and extra training to more providers. The key point is that there is no inexpensive way to care properly for our babies and children. Either we have to do it ourselves or we have to expect to pay a great deal to have others do it. To try to get away with paying for the most important work in the world with minimal wages is a mistake that will undermine the development of future generations.

Improve Funding for Day Care

For families who can't afford expensive child care because they are working just to get food on the table, we must have robust federal, state, and community-level programs that can subsidize the highest quality possible. This is especially needed for babies and children emerging from generations of poverty. In order to have an equal opportunity to succeed, they need *optimal*-quality care, not poor- or even average-quality care. Federal, state, and community subsidies cannot support the care of every child, but this assistance is vitally needed for children from low-income families. Unfortunately, under welfare reform, federal and state governments are legally able to pay child-care providers and centers only pitifully small amounts to care for the children of former welfare recipients. In some states, child-care providers earn as little as $20 a day to care for an infant or toddler. Because of a loophole in the 1996 welfare reform act, states are required to submit a plan to the federal government showing how they will adjust their payments to child-care providers and centers to reflect the market-rate wages—but they are not required ever to *implement* those plans![2] Closing this loophole so that states are required to use their federal funds to pay child-care providers better-than-market-rate wages should be high on the priority list as legislators and public policy analysts begin to look toward reauthorization of the welfare reform act in 2002.

Improve Caregivers' Training

Another critical component that needs to be improved in order to achieve consistency and quality of care is training programs. Caregivers who are learning on the job with in-service training and for whom increased knowledge can lead to higher wages and higher status will do a better job, feel better about themselves, and, in many instances, make a longer-term commitment to the profession of caregiver. In-service training programs not only motivate caregivers but also help them interact with children in developmentally appropriate ways. As we discussed in Chapter 3, as children grow and develop, their needs change. At four months, they require nurturing, wooing relationships; by eight months, they're already requiring lots of back-and-forth interactions; by 15 months, they need a helpful problem solver; by two and three years of age, they need a pretend-play partner; and by three and four years of age, they need a debater and opinion seeker to help them develop their logical thinking skills. To be able to engage children's minds in these differing ways requires not only dedication on the part of caregivers but also training in child development and coaching by senior staff—and a smaller number of children for them to care for.

Training would also help caregivers tailor their interactions to the individual differences of the child. The child who is sensitive to touch and sounds requires more energized, yet regulated, caregiving interactions than one with less sensitivity in these areas. The child with strong language, but a weak sense of where things are in space requires different types of interactions than a child with the opposite pattern. Focusing on individual differences allows us to tailor care to the child. If we are to expect such sensitivity and insight from caregivers, we need to make it possible for them to obtain further training.

Encourage Parental Involvement

Another feature that's important to focus on in improving day care is better working relationships between parents and day-care staff. As we saw in Chapter 6, parents and caregivers must see themselves as partners with supportive communication patterns. Too often we see, instead, lack of communication, covert rivalries or put-downs, and blaming. In order to provide a collaborative, supportive context, day-care staff need training on how to work with parents. For instance, caregivers need to maintain a special availability at the end of the day so that they can offer reassurance to as well as exchange information with tired parents when they come to fetch their children. Busy, overworked, stressed day-care staff will find this hard to offer when they do not have time to meet among themselves and receive no administrative support. Once again, proper wages, better teacher-to-children ratios, and training will help in creating a respectful relationship.

A More Nurturing Daily Schedule

In addition, the daily schedule for children in day care needs adjustment if they are to have an opportunity for healthy emotional and intellectual growth. Whether at home or in day care, there are three types of interactions that should characterize a baby's or child's play: direct play, cuddling, or games; activity in which a caregiver facilitates the child's exploration of the environment, by offering blocks or crayons, answering questions, helping to find toys, and so forth; and independent activity, where the caregiver is present and available, but the child busies himself or herself with a toy or other interest.

The direct interaction should occur for about 20 minutes or more at least four times a day, and needs to be one-on-one. In addition, of course, day care affords toddlers and young children opportunities for play with peers. No more than one third of the baby's or toddler's day should be spent in fully independent play, and this should be only for short periods of time. As is obvious, structuring the child's day in this manner requires both more staff time and training than now is available at most centers.

Some may see these improvements as onerous and costly—but remember, they are for our children. Private college now can easily cost $30,000-plus a year, and parents plan for decades to be able to pay their children's tuition. Yet the early years are even more important than the college ones. We mustn't continue to neglect or undervalue this most important time in our own and our children's lives.

9

Solutions for Corporations and Governments

P olicies of corporations and state and federal governments play a crucial role in either supporting or
undermining the way families care for their children. I argued earlier in this book that families and societies seem to have separated
into two divergent paths. One path dictates that people master
and conquer their environment—the "survival of the fittest"
approach—which arose from primitive experience, where we
learned how to prevail in the face of the complicated, often hos-
tile, world. This pugnacious view of the world still has useful
applications in our more modern times. There are still challenges—economic, scientific, political—to master. But the
approach becomes counterproductive when it ignores the other
side of evolution and disregards the consequences of doing so.
Humans have evolved not only through competition, but also
through cooperation and nurturing, which make them adapted
for living successfully in complex social groups. When success is
measured only in terms of winners and losers, of who gets the
most money and who doesn't, other values suffer and the glue
that holds society together weakens.

Employment Policies

Our private industry needs to shift from a primarily short-term profit-driven ethos to one that balances competition with responsibility toward future generations. To ensure a supply of successful members of the workforce, the business community must create work policies that are supportive of children and families. Such policies recognize that human societies require citizens who have been nurtured to work in groups and parent future generations. Nurturing care is the less celebrated but in many respects more essential aspect of evolutionary adaptation than competition.

Child- and family-centered employment policies need four critical elements:

1. Reasonable parental-leave policies for mothers and/or fathers immediately after the birth of a new baby. Ideally, corporate parental-leave policies would allow a parent to spend most of that year at home.
2. Opportunities for part-time and flextime work arrangements for parents. Many businesses already know that a two-thirds- or three-fourths-time employee often accomplishes as much or more, proportionally, than a full-time employee. The sense that work hours are limited can lead to greater work efficiency. Jobs must be redefined in terms of "scope" so that flexible work schedules or part-time schedules can be worked out.
3. Health and mental-health insurance and related services. These must cover part-time (over a certain number of hours) as well as full-time workers.
4. On-site, high-quality child care, when the business is large enough, for those who require it.

Corporations need to be involved in reclaiming a nurturing ethic within our society for families and communities—even though they may seem like unlikely candidates for this role! Corporate policies can help employees and communities care for children and can encourage the close-knit structures that make the family the critical social unit for nurturing children and providing stability for society. Enlightened corporations will incorporate into business practices the knowledge that families need support if their offspring are to develop the intellectual, social, and emotional capacities needed in both managers and a competent workforce.

There are those who would argue that corporations need the financial freedom to cut jobs and benefits so as to remain economically viable. Otherwise, the argument goes, there would be no jobs, no workplace, and, therefore, no way that families could support their children, let alone reclaim their care. Naturally, we can't ignore those facts, and any suggestions that would affect the workplace need to be balanced with these constraints. At the same time, an enlightened position toward the family is, in a sense, self-serving and, from a long-term perspective, economically justifiable if it helps create a productive, creative, industrious workforce.

We are talking about a long-term view. In a world driven by quarterly financial returns, that's a hard view for companies' managers to take; in such a world, companies have little incentive to inquire how their marketing strategies or workplace policies will affect the next generation, and even beyond. The same goes for politicians. Getting them to focus on a generation of voters who haven't even been born is extraordinarily difficult or, for the vast majority of public officials, actually impossible.

But we have no choice. We simply must devote a portion of our energies to longer-term planning if we wish to remain viable as a nation. Companies need to function as full members of their

communities, providing a full range of support services to families (as some more enlightened employers now do). These include
substance-abuse counseling, family counseling, and programs
that teach workers how to cope with work stress as well as other
domestic pressures on them.

The corporate world has taken some steps toward these goals,
but it needs to do much more. One corporate leader I know
points out that even in these more egalitarian times, many high-
level corporate chieftains have spouses who remain in the home
to raise the children. He notes that such managers end up with a
distorted view of the world, that it becomes easy for them to
assume that wives can afford to stay home and that male workers
must devote long hours to the job at the expense of their families.
In fact, he points out, "Our best people tend to be people who
have other commitments." He has found that qualities needed in
employees in order to achieve corporate success "are no longer
obedience and punching the time clock." Rather, it is sophisticated thinking, and high-level reasoning that must be nurtured
in employees.

Another corporate chief, who heads a billion-dollar company
that employs thousands of minimum-wage workers throughout
the country, embodies the challenges facing companies today if
they decide to devote some resources to family-friendly policies.
His company was in the midst of setting up an on-site day-care
center at its headquarters, at a cost of $800,000, when it was
acquired by an out-of-state firm. Plans for the child-care center
were dropped when the company's headquarters were shifted out
of state, he said.

On the plus side, this same corporation has instituted flextime
scheduling at its workplace sites, allowing employees to work six-
hour shifts, to get more time at home every day, or longer daily
shifts, if they want to get more off-duty days to spend with their

families. This corporate chief, significantly, has young children and could see the benefits that the company's policies offer families and children. But he saw the shift to flextime also as a smart dollars-and-cents move. In an economy where there are labor shortages in some industries, this executive said he saw the policy as key to the company's future success.

"We think it's a win/win situation," he said. "With the labor market the way it is, the companies that will win in the years ahead are the ones who are listening to, and serving, their three key constituents—their customers, obviously, and their owners, but also their employees serving the customers and owners." In other words, he says, serving employees is good for business.

That outlook is certainly laudable, and if everyone thought that way, there would be no reason for concern. But everyone doesn't. This man was an exception. First, this executive was sympathetic to his time-strapped employees because he has two young children himself and saw the need to appeal to employees in a tight labor market. But what happens in firms where top executives don't have young children and so aren't as sympathetic to the concerns of their workers and to changing conditions in a slower economy, one in which there is no labor shortage? Family-friendly workplace policies will be vulnerable as companies struggle to compete. That's where government needs to step in.

State and National Policies

Our laws are slowly—too slowly—moving in the direction of recognizing the crucial role that the nurturing side of humanity's nature plays in our development, and our future. The Family and Medical Leave Act of 1993, which mandates that employees of companies with more than 50 employees be permitted to take unpaid time to care for a child or other family members, recognizes the need to rebalance our priorities. But this is not enough to stem the movement that is undermining our ability to care adequately for our children and ourselves.

First and foremost, improving policies for children and families in children's younger years requires a change in attitude. When opponents of increasing spending on day care say that providing high-quality day care is too expensive, or when they protest that asking parents to give up full-time careers for part-time ones is too hard on parents, the question that needs to be asked is this: too expensive or too hard compared to what? Most complicated challenges can't be solved easily or inexpensively. If we continue to assume that the only viable solutions to our current dilemma are easy or inexpensive, only one outcome can be guaranteed: The problem won't be solved.

The real challenge is to recognize that properly caring for children will be *neither* easy nor cheap.

One parallel is to consider the resources that our country pours into military spending in the name of self-defense. The question posed on the old poster that you sometimes see on school walls still rings true: "What if the schools had all the money they need, and the army had to hold a bake sale to buy a bomber?" As a country, we take for granted that sophisticated machinery and technology for war weaponry cost billions of dollars, and that this is the price we pay for the future safety of our country. But we do not recognize that the future strength and security of our country depends on the quality of care we provide for our children now.

Among the large-scale changes that must be made if children's and parents' needs are to be met are the following:

• *Tax breaks and other governmental incentives to private companies that institute family-friendly policies.* Targeted deductions and incentives are needed to give private industry the will to offer more flexible work schedules, longer parental leave times, and better insurance coverage for all.

• *Education programs that fund the teaching of human development in our schools, beginning in grade school and extending through college.* These programs would give as much weight to explaining the emotional and mental side of our development as to humans' physical development. A bias against mental health concerns is a bias against the family.

• *Improvements in the quality of day care through direct subsidies and other incentives.* Bigger and better-funded programs are needed to improve the quality of child care for those who need it. As we said earlier, this is especially needed for low-income and single parents who have no choice but to use day care. At-risk children and families must be the first priority for improved child care. Early assessments and interventions need to be funded and built into the child-care system. As discussed in Chapter 8, we need to improve teacher-to-child ratios—to, for example, three babies for one caregiver instead of the current standard ratio of four babies for every caregiver.

Moreover, for babies who must spend long hours in day care we may need to lower that ratio to two babies per caregiver and add extra nurturing time throughout the day, especially in the late afternoon. As indicated earlier, there is mounting evidence that long days in group settings are stressful for very young children. As children become toddlers and preschoolers, the ratios for those who are in full day care must also be improved.   ·

In addition, we need to expand in-service training programs; and to raise salaries and improve supervision and program support. We need to change child-care center policies so that the same caregivers stay with the same group of children through infancy and the preschool years. All this requires both higher performance standards and increased funding.

• *Welfare policy that factors in support of, and time for, mothers to care for their young children themselves.* Mothers of children under the age of three should be able to work half-time, or in two-adult households, parents should be able to work two-thirds time. Parents should also be provided with help in learning parenting skills if they need it. Indeed, the goal of welfare reform should be fourfold. It must provide parents with (1) employment, (2) work skills, (3) opportunities to care for their own children, and (4) where needed, help with improving their child-rearing skills.

• *Funding to help communities take responsibility for providing every child with nurturing relationships—even children whose nuclear families may not be able to provide them.* Some families need considerable help to meet the needs of their children. Families in which there is drug use, poverty, or mental health problems, as well as families where children are abused or neglected will require a wide range of support services. Provision of these services needs to be subsidized. Community services that can effectively nurture children from even the most troubled families must be made available. Such services would resemble a village or neighborhood, where each adult takes sympathetic interest in everyone's child. But it could also be a large apartment complex or a city block, perhaps. Unlike urban housing projects from which the most functional residents have fled, leaving the most troubled and poverty-stricken families behind, an ideal "vertical village" would have a range of residents: some extremely troubled families, some households with adults either on welfare or working who function quite well, some adults without children, and some older members of this community. Within this "village," a well-staffed, well-equipped infant and child facility that would accept children from birth could be used by parents from troubled families as well as single parents or couples in which both partners need to work to put bread on the table. In this kind of community, a child-care center is useful and, indeed, crucial. The child care would need to incorporate care that recognized the six essential milestones that children master on their way to healthy emotional and intellectual development. Rather than waiting to intervene after a child has begun to have difficulties, staff would step in early to maximize each baby's developmental changes.

To attract residents to this diverse community, a variety of financial incentives would be needed—for example, subsidized rents, reduced day-care fees, and educational opportunities. Only a large-scale commitment by city, state, or the federal government would make this possible.

International Policies

Globally, the United States lags behind almost every developed nation when it comes to national family policies that encourage working parents to spend time at home with their young children. Only a few countries have gone as far as is needed for the optimum development of the world's youngest generations. Italy, for example, offers most working mothers five months' paid maternity leave and an additional six months at lower levels of cash benefits. In France, as of this writing working mothers get 16 weeks' maternity benefits at nearly full pay for their first and second child and 24 weeks of mostly paid leave for subsequent children. In addition, they can take up to three years of unpaid parental leave with job protection.[1] Many union agreements call for additional paid maternity leave for certain workers.[2] Austria offers 16 weeks' paid maternity leave for mothers, and mothers are also eligible for up to three years' leave with some portion of their salaries paid.[3] In Britain, any woman who has been on the job more than a year gets almost 30 weeks of leave with a guaranteed return to the same job level, and newly hired women get at least 18 weeks, with a guaranteed return to the same job level. Employers are not required to pay, but many provide compensation.[4] Germany gives 14 weeks of family leave after the birth of a baby, and mothers can extend that leave at reduced pay for two to three years.[5]

The Scandinavian countries have a reputation for providing generous family-leave benefits—and deservedly so. Sweden offers 12 months of maternity or paternity leave paid at 85 percent of a parent's salary.[6] Its policy also includes the right to a reduced workday until a child is eight. In Norway there exists a wide range of generous family-leave policies that enable both parents to combine part-time work and partial family-leave benefits. For example, one parent can take leave at full salary for eight months and then another parent can combine 80 percent work and 20 percent leave for almost two more years. In recent years, the government has added policies that encourage fathers to stay home with their children for a while. As a result, paternal leave increased from 4 percent in 1993 to 70 percent by 1995.[7]

Although Canada's family policies are not as good as those of many European countries, they are still better than those of the United States. Our northern neighbor offers 15 weeks of maternity leave and 10 weeks of parental leave, funded at about one-half salary up to a weekly ceiling.[8]

Political Priorities

Domestically, our first priority is to get parents home with young children, even if it means fewer working parents, lower earnings for the families, and lower tax revenues because of their lower earnings. The government must embrace this new ethic. For the last several decades, we have been drifting away from the belief that babies and preschool children belong at home with their families. Indeed, we have been moving away from that assumption since the Great Depression, which put us in touch with our collective vulnerability.

Unfortunately, the debate about these issues in Washington and in state legislatures around the county has evolved into unproductive arguments between liberals and conservatives that are getting us nowhere. Each side mixes priorities with politics. The politics tend to pit working parents against at-home parents and heighten concerns about gender equity and equality. Both sides of the political spectrum need to work together on the solutions our country requires. These solutions are the ones that will help put children first, provide special support for families and children in need, enable parents to spend more time caring for their children, and improve the quality of out-of-home care for those who require it.

We all must recognize that when we have children to raise, we can't do it all. We can't work twelve-hour days and provide the nurturing our infants, toddlers, and preschoolers require. Consequently, we must set some priorities, and the federal government as well as local governments and businesses must help parents by making it possible for them to work part-time and also have access to high-quality child care for their children. In other words, what is needed is not an either/or solution but one that provides families with good options to care for their children themselves and to find trustworthy out-of-home care when they need it.

As people across the political spectrum search for solutions to the child-care dilemma, they must set aside political calculations and put sincere concern for children and families at center stage. As was argued in Chapter 1, we tend to deny our own vulnerability and, therefore, the needs of our children. Yet our awareness is not far from the surface. We know, for example, on an individual basis, that should illness strike someone in our own family, we quickly take our eye off the stock market and begin valuing the basics of a warm touch, a smile, and an embrace. Indeed, sometimes it takes fear to put us in touch with the core of our humanity. Collectively, we also tend to lose sight of our need for one another when things are going relatively well. But times of relative affluence are precisely when we are more able to pay attention to the needs of our children and families.

As we have seen in this book, putting children first requires far-reaching solutions. These will be neither inexpensive nor easy and will require effort at the individual, community, corporate, and government levels. But no other investment of time or money will have a more immediate and rewarding effect, and also have a greater long-term benefit for future generations.

Notes

Chapter 1

1. National Center for Education Statistics, "Characteristics of Children's Early Care and Education Programs," June 1998, data from Sandra L. Hoffert, Kimberlee A. Shavman, Robert Henke, and Jerry West, National Household Education Survey, 1995, NCES publication 98-128 (Washington, D.C.: NCES, 1998).

2. Centers for Disease Control and Prevention, "Rates of Homicide, Suicide and Firearm-Related Death Among Children—26 Industrialized Countries," *Morbidity and Mortality Weekly Report,* 7 Feb. 1997.

Chapter 2

1. National Academy of Sciences, Board on Children, Youth and Families, "From Neurons to Neighborhoods: The Science of Early Childhood Development," 2000, p. 9.

2. S. Helburn et al., "Cost, Quality and Child Outcomes Study," public report, University of Colorado–Denver, Economics Department, 1995.

3. NICHD Early Child Care Research Network, "Characteristics and Quality of Childcare for Toddlers and Preschoolers," *Applied Developmental Science* 4(3):116–135.

4. Ellen Galinsky, Carolee Howes, Susan Kontos, and Marybeth Shinn, "The Study of Children in Family Child Care and Relative Care," report (New York: Families and Work Institute, 1994).

5. Child Care Employee Project, California Policy Seminar, University of California, November, 1991.

6. B. Fuller and S. L. Kagan, *Remember the Children: Mothers Balance Work and Child Care Under Welfare Reform,* Wave 1 Report, Growing Up in Poverty Project 2000 (Berkeley, Calif.: University of California–Berkeley, 2000).

7. NICHD Early Child Care Research Network, "Children in Working Poor Families," submitted to *Child Development.*

8. Kathryn Taafe Young, Katherine White Marsland, Edward Zigler, "The Regulatory Status of Center-Based Infant and Toddler Child Care," *American Journal of Orthopsychiatry* 67(October 1997):535–44.

9. M. Whitehouse, "Making Work Pay in the Child Care Industry: Promising Practices for Improving Compensation," Center for the Child Care Workforce, 1995 (www.ccw.org).

10. "Eased Day-Care Rules; Virginia Committee Seeks to Attract More Workers, *Washington Post*, 17 Oct. 1997, p. B1.

11. NICHD Early Child Care Research Network, "Early Child Care and Self-Control, Compliance and Problem Behavior at Twenty-Four and Thirty-Six Months," *Child Development* 69(1998):1145–70; ibid., "Effect Sizes from the NICHD Study of Early Child Care," Paper presented at the Biennial Meeting of the Society for Research in Child Development, Albuquerque, N.M., April 1999; ibid., "The Relation of Child Care to Cognitive and Language Development," *Child Development* 71(2000):960–80.

12. Such studies include the Carolina Abecedarian Study, the Yale Child Welfare Research Program, and the Perry Preschool Project. These studies followed young children or infants who had received high-quality care into adulthood and compared their outcomes against young children who had not received such care. These studies are discussed further in Edward F. Zigler and Nancy W. Hall, *Child Development and Social Policy* (New York: McGraw-Hill, 2000).

13. Institute for Research on Poverty, "Child Care Quality: Does It Matter and Does It Need to Be Improved?," University of Wisconsin–Madison, April 2000.

14. "The Children of the 'Cost, Quality and Outcomes' Study Go to School," University of North Carolina–Chapel Hill, June 1999.

15. NICHD Early Childhood Research Network, "Quality Child Care and Child Development Prior to School," paper presented by Deborah Lowe Vandell at the meeting of the Society for Research in Child Development, Minneapolis, 19–22 April 2001.

16. NICHD Early Childhood Research Network, "Early Child Care and Children's Development Prior to School Entry," paper presented at the meeting of the Society for Research in Child Development, Minneapolis, 19–22 April 2001.

17. Ibid., "Child Care and Mother Care Interaction in the First Three Years of Life," *Developmental Psychology* 35(1999):1399–1413.

18. Ibid., "The Effects of Infant Child Care on Infant-Mother Attachment Security," *Child Development* 68(5):860–79.

19. Ibid., "Interactions of Child Care and Family Risk in Relation to Child Development at 15, 24, and 36 Months," submitted to *Development and Psychopathology*.

20. D.L. Vandell and M.A. Corsanti, "Variations in Early Child Care: Do They Predict Subsequent Social, Emotional and Cognitive Differences?" *Early Childhood Research Quarterly*, 1990.

21. Personal communication, Megan R. Gunnar, Ph.D., director of the study, at the Institute of Child Development, University of Minnesota, Minneapolis, MN.

22. Personal correspondence, Pnina Klein, professor, Department of Education, Bar Ilan University, Israel.

23. National Center for Education Statistics, U.S. Department of Education, "Characteristics of Children's Early Care and Education Programs: Data from the 1995 National Household Education Survey Report 98–128" (Washington, D.C.: NCES, June 1998.

24. "The Realities of Day Care; National Institute of Child Health and Human Development's Study of Early Child Care," *The Public Interest*, Sept. 1996.

25. National Center for Education Statistics, U.S. Department of Education, "Characteristics of Children's Early Care and Education Programs, 1995."

26. Stanley Greenspan, M.D., *The Growth of the Mind* (Cambridge, Mass.: Perseus, 1997); ibid., *Building Healthy Minds* (Cambridge, Mass.: Perseus, 1999); Stanley Greenspan and T. Berry Brazelton, M.D., *The Irreducible Needs of Children* (Cambridge, Mass.: Perseus, 2000).

27. Bureau of Labor Statistics, "Preschool Teachers and Child-Care Workers," *Occupational Outlook Handbook*, 2000–1 ed. (Washington, D.C.: Department Labor, 2000).

28. Urban Institute, "Who's Caring for Our Youngest Children? Child Care Patterns of Infants and Toddlers," Urban Institute online article, OP-42. Available: www.urban.org/socwelfare.htm#children.

29. "Good Day Care Found to Aid Cognitive Skills of Children," AP, *New York Times*, 5 April 1997, A12.

30. "How Good Is Your Child Care?" *Child*, October 1997, p. 106.

31. "Day Care Offers Reassurance to Working Parents," *Washington Post*, 4 April 1997, A1.

32. Dr. Katherine Booth of the University of Washington, address at the Annual Meeting of the Society for the Advancement of Science, Seattle, 26 January 1999.

33. Some may disagree with my conclusion. In order to support the notion that average out-of-home care may be adequate, they may cite data on the relationship between quality of care and assessments of aspects of language and cognitive functioning that were part of a "school readiness" assessment. The following pattern relating scores on school readiness assessments to quality and type of child care was found:

High-quality child care: 47.2 (school readiness score)

High average child care: 43.4

Low average child care: 39.5

Low-quality child care: 38.6

Maternal care of all types (high-, middle-, and low-quality combined): 43.6

As can be seen, high-quality care is associated with strong scores, and lower-quality care is associated with weaker scores. Exclusive maternal care of high-, average-, and low-quality care combined was similar to high average out-of-home care. Unfortunately, there were no analyses comparing high-quality maternal care and the different qualities of out-of-home child care. In addition, the difference between low average child care and high average, while in the expected direction, was not statistically significant.

The similarity between high average child care and all types of maternal care and the lack of statistical significance between high average and low average child care on school readiness scores might tempt one to mistakenly conclude that average child care is "adequate."

Such a conclusion, I believe, goes beyond the existing data. To make a judgment that current average care is "adequate," we would need additional data. We would need a breakdown of the quality of care provided by parents (that is, how much parental care is high, average, or low quality). Parents who could provide high-quality care, where positive caregiving was very characteristic, would not be likely to deem "adequate" average care where positive caregiving is somewhat uncharacteristic or only somewhat characteristic. In addition, to make such a judgment we would need longitudinal data in regard to the effects of full-time day care on in-depth emotional and social functioning such as the capacity for stable relationships, intimacy, healthy empathy, parenting, responsible community membership, etc. As indicated earlier, such data are not available and cannot be predicted from the very limited measures of social behavior at age 4 and a half, the age for which the NICHD study has its most recent data at this writing.

34. NICHD Early Child Care Research Network, "The Interaction of Child Care and Family Risk in Relation to Child Development at 15, 24, and 36 Months," submitted to *Journal of Applied Developmental Science*.

Chapter 3

1. See Stanley I. Greenspan, *The Growth of the Mind* (Cambridge, Mass: Perseus, 1997).

2. Ibid., *Building Healthy Minds* (Cambridge, Mass.: Perseus, 1999).

3. E. Tronick, H. Als, L. Adamson, S. Wise, and T. B. Brazelton, "The Infant's Response to Entrapment Between Contradicting Messages in Face-to-Face Interaction," *Journal of the Academy of Child Psychiatry* 17 (1978):1–13.

Chapter 7

1. See notes 1 and 2 in Chapter 1.
2. Stanley I. Greenspan, *Growth of the Mind* (Cambridge, Mass: Perseus, 1997).
3. Ibid., *Building Healthy Minds* (Cambridge Mass.: Perseus, 1999).

Chapter 8

1. Personal correspondence, February 2001, Marcy Whitebrook, director, Center for Industrial Policy, University of California–Berkeley.
2. "Alexandria Seeks Fairer Child-Care Subsidy," *Washington Post*, 15 May 2001, B5.

Chapter 9

1. Canadian Policy Research Networks Inc., *Comparative Family Policy: Eight Countries' Stories* (Ottawa: Ottawa & Renouf, 1998).
2. Interview with Sheila Kammerman, professor of social policy and planning, Columbia University, New York City, September 1999.
3. Edward Zigler and Nancy W. Hall, *Child Development and Social Policy* (New York: McGraw-Hill, 1999), p. 64.
4. T. R. Reid, "In England, Another Victory for Labor," *Washington Post*, 28 March 2000, A24.
5. Zigler and Hall, *Child Development and Social Policy*, p. 64; Canadian Policy Research Networks Inc., *Comparative Family Policy*, p. 11.
6. Zigler and Hall, *Child Development and Social Policy*, p. 16.
7. Canadian Policy Research Networks Inc., "Comparative Family Policy," p. 14.
8. Zigler and Hall, *Child Development and Social Policy*, p. 9.

Acknowledgments

I would like to express my appreciation to my wife Nancy, and my colleagues Serena Wieder and the late Reginald Lourie for their collaboration in understanding children and parents; to Sarah Miller and Jan Tunney for supporting the children and families in my practice; and to Merloyd Lawrence for her sensitive and insightful editing and suggestions.

Index

About the Authors

Stanley I. Greenspan, M.D., is Clinical Professor of Psychiatry, Behavioral Sciences, and Pediatrics, George Washington University Medical School and a practicing child psychiatrist. A supervising child psychoanalyst at the Washington Psychoanalytic Institute in Washington, D.C., and Chairman of the Interdisciplinary Council on Developmental and Learning Disorders, he was previously Chief of the Mental Health Study Center and Director of the Clinical Infant Developmental Program at the National Institute of Mental Health. Among his many national honors, he has received the Ittleson Prize, the American Psychiatric Association's highest award for child psychiatry research. He also received the Blanche F. Ittleson award from the American Orthopsychiatric Association for outstanding contributions to American mental health, making him the first individual to receive both Ittleson prizes. His work has been featured on PBS in a *Nova* documentary, "Life's First Feelings" and ABC, NCB; and CBS news; on ABC's *Nightline*; on PBS's *News Hour*; and in stories in *Time*, *Newsweek*, the *New York Times*, and *The Washington Post*.

A founder and former president of ZERO TO THREE: The National Center for Infants, Toddlers, and Families, Dr. Greenspan is the author of more than one hundred scholarly articles and chapters and is the author or editor of over thirty books for both scholarly and general audiences. His pioneering works, which have been translated into over a dozen languages, include *The Growth of the Mind* (with Beryl Lieff Benderly), *Building Healthy Minds* (with Nancy Breslau Lewis), *The Child with Special Needs* (with Serena Wieder, Ph.D. and Robin Simon), *The Irreducible Needs of Children* (with T. Berry Brazelton, M.D.), *Infancy and Early Childhood, Intelligence and Adaptation: An Integration of Psychoanalytic and Piagetian Developmental Psychology, First Feelings* (with Nancy Thorndike Greenspan), and *Playground Politics* and *The Challenging Child* (both with Jacqueline Salmon).

Jaqueline L. Salmon is a staff writer for the Washington Post, where she covers family issues, and an on-line columnist for washingtonpost.com. She is the co-author of "Playground Politics" and "The Challenging Child," and has written for numerous publications, including *GQ, MS., Self, Glamour,* and *American Baby*. She lives in the Washington D.C. area with her husband and two children.